An Englishman in Texas

Raul Idevey
GOD BLESS YOU
(0-1-18

An Englishman in Texas

A MEMOIR
BY RON KENNEY

with Kimberly Parish Davis

Madville Publishing LLC
Madisonville, Texas

Printed in the United States of America

FIRST EDITION
Requests for permission to reproduce material from this work should be sent to:

    Permissions
    Madville Publishing LLC
    P.O. Box 207
    Madisonville, TX 77864

ACKNOWLEDGMENTS

Thanks to all the people who have helped me in my life: to Mr. Heath for putting up with me through my bad times; to Mr. & Mrs. Smith for giving me a loving home; to my sister Doris for getting me to the USA; to Mr. Arthur Tinner for getting me a job at Tommy Oliphant's; to Buster Parish and Pat Cole for all they did for me in more ways than one; to Doc Williams for getting me the job with Mr. Mecom; to the Turner girls who fed me dinner at Jack Frost for 3 weeks till I got a paycheck; to Tom Mackey who got me a job at the tin smelter; to Don Hanson, Mr. Davis, and Gene Felter for getting me on the crew at Amoco; and to the Hayes family for all they have done for me.

Cover Design by Jacqueline Davis
Author Photograph by Alice Kenney

ISBN: 978-1-948692-02-1 paperback, and 978-1-948692-03-8 ebook
Library of Congress Control Number: 2018948234

Dedicated to:

God and to the life he gave me and
to the everlasting life to come.

Table of Contents

GALLWAY RACES

There where the racecourse is
Delight makes all of the one mind
The riders upon the swift horses
The field that closes in behind.
We too had good attendance once,
Hearers, hearteners of the work,
Aye, horsemen for companions
Before the merchant and the clerk
Breathed on the world with timid breath;
But some day and at some new moon
We'll learn that sleeping is not death
Hearing the whole earth change its tune,
Flesh being wild again, and it again
Crying aloud as the racecourse is;
And find hearteners among men
That ride upon horses.

—*W. B. Yeats*

An Englishman in Texas

Introduction

I have known Ron Kenney all my life. He says the first time he saw me, I was a tiny baby in my mother's arms. My mother says I was asleep on a pillow on the seat of the pickup truck, but my mother always remembers me as that baby on a pillow as she bounced across some pasture rescuing some horse or another. Horses were central to my parents' lives then, on a goat and sheep ranch in Junction, Texas. It seems an unlikely place to breed race horses, but that is where their first race horse was born in 1960—the same year I was born. I think the race horse part was serendipity. Daddy traded somebody for a stud horse named Hobo Adam, a magnificent animal that sired a filly my mother called Bo's Hope.

I have no idea how they worked out that the filly could run—I was a baby at the time—but they decided they needed someone to help them get her ready for the track. And that is when Ron entered our lives. He had recently arrived in this country, and he was willing to take whatever work he could get—even riding a spoiled pet of a Quarter Horse.

For the purposes of this book, my family only appears at the points where our paths have crossed with Ron's, and I wouldn't have mentioned them quite as many times as Ron does, but it is his story. I am merely the editor.

This project began about ten years ago when Ron asked me to help him write his life story. I was fascinated. I've always been fascinated by Ron's life, so we started recording conversations on my back porch. I scanned a lot of his photos, and my good friend and sometimes clerical assistant Alisha Badillo spent many hours transcribing recorded conversations. More recently, I've been fortunate to have the assistance of my daughter, Jacqui Davis, and my favorite proofreader, Elizabeth Evans. We've all been privileged to work on this book and to get to know Ron in the process.

Ron has an infectious enthusiasm about him. As he tells the story of his life, it becomes clear that his intuition and his gregarious nature have seen him through situations that would have broken lesser men. His life hasn't been easy, but when he tells the stories, always with a smile and a twinkle in his eye, he makes it sound easy. He doesn't flinch at his faults, and shares those right along with his triumphs.

This is Ron Kenney as he appears in my earliest memories of him.

One of my favorite memories of Ron is of a time when I was seven or eight years old. It was always a treat when he came to our house, because he brought such good energy with him. He would pay attention to lowly little me. On this day, he turned his attention my way and asked what I liked to do. What sorts of games did I like to play? Did I enjoy riding my bike? It had been a few years since I had seen him, so we were getting acquainted again. I told Ron that I rode my bike all the time. And that was all he needed. Next thing I knew, we were borrowing a bike from a friend's big sister and off we went! I was delighted that a grown-up would take the time to ride bikes with me, that he seemed to be having a great time zooming around the neighborhood and through the empty parking lot of the nearby grocery store.

I've gotten to know Ron as an adult, and now I can tell that he carries that positive outlook into all of his encounters with others—or nearly all of his encounters with others. He repeatedly tells of people who have been good to him, and while there are not many of them, he tells of the ones who were not so good to him. I don't think I'd like to be on that list of the ones who treated him poorly. Ron offers an example of the right way to live. He makes people happy. I hope that you will recognize that in the way we have chosen to tell his story, and I hope you enjoy reading that story as much as I have enjoyed recording it.

—Kimberly Parish Davis
Madisonville, Texas
May 2018

Chapter 1—Early Childhood

I was born in 1930, on the first of August, at little place called Dipton, England, #1 Curry Square.[1] My father was a coal miner, and his name was Joseph Hall Clark Kenney.

My mother's maiden name was Mary Elisabeth Larmouth. She was a Catholic until she was seventeen when she married my Dad, then she joined the Salvation Army. She was chosen from among all the Salvation Army singers to represent them at the Royal Albert Hall in London where she sang for William Booth, the Salvation Army founder. I met God in the Salvation Army with my mother and I

---

1   According to Victor T.D. Holliday in his "Walking in my Fore-father's Footsteps," a history of Dipton written for the Durham County Council, "The first map showing the name Dipton was recorded in 1625. The village was shown as being a long straggling place, much the same as it is today. The centre of the village of Dipton was originally known as Collierley Dykes, meaning the pits among the trees and hedges." http://www.durhamintime.org.uk/durham_miner/walking.pdf

give God and my mother the credit for my singing, which I have continued throughout my life.

Mother's family came from Scotland and my father's family came from Ireland. I've been told by the rest of the family that my mother's part of the family was Spanish. My ancestor was apparently on one of the ships from the Armada sent by King Philip II of Spain in 1588 to invade England. The story goes that his ship got away and made it to Scotland where my fore-father stayed and married a Scottish girl. That's where the Larmouths came from as far as I know.

I was the youngest of nine Kenney children: Joseph Clark (the first), Elizabeth, Rosaline, Annabel, Frank, William, Doris, Albert, and Ronald. I know that the last three of us did not have middle names.

Our Dipton house didn't have electricity, only gas for lighting, but if we didn't have money to put in the meter, we didn't have gas either. We lit our way to bed with a candle. The cooking stove was coal fired, and there was no running water in the house. Mama kept a great big cast iron pot beside the stove. The pot was always filled with hot water for washing the dishes and the clothes. It never moved. We filled our bath with water from that same cast iron pot every Saturday night. Upstairs was the master bedroom and one other big room for all of us kids. Girls and boys slept in the same room because that's just the way it was.

Ron's father, Joseph Hall Clark Kenney, who made his living as a coal miner in County Durham, England.

When I was four years old I went to school. We would call it pre-school now. I recall one time we were going to have a parade. We were made to wear sailor uniforms with red, white and blue pom-poms on the shoes. We made the little pom-poms from the cardboard tops that came in the top of milk bottles to celebrate King Edward who was going to be crowned as the new king of England. Well, as we all know now, he abdicated so he could marry an American woman named Mrs. Simpson and never became king. Instead, his brother George was crowned in 1936. He was the father of our current Queen Elizabeth. She took the throne when her father died in 1952.

Number 9 Front Street, Little Town, Durham. This photo shows Ron's sister Elizabeth's children.

But back in 1934, I was just a little boy when the Dipton coal mine closed down, and we later learned that they could not keep the water out of it,[2] so that put my dad out of work, and we had to move to #9 Front Street, Littletown, Durham. This house had three bedrooms and a flush toilet outside, but we still did not have electricity.

---

2   The "New Delight" mine closed down in 1940 "due partly to the escalating costs to mine the coal and also to the Second World War closing the foreigh markets it served." There were, however several pits in operation in the area, and Ron's father worked in the Sherbard HIll Mine. http://www.durhamintime.org.uk/durham_miner/walking.pdf

The Problem of Drainage in the Coal Mines

Water has to constantly be removed from coal mines, and drainage becomes increasingly problematic as shallow collieries with natural drainage play out and it becomes necessary to follow seams to ever greater depths.

Sites where gravity tunnels could be utilized quickly became exhausted as mines were pushed ever deeper beneath Earth's surface. In the latter half of the 1600s, mine proprietors devised more creative ways of removing water from their mines. Multiple levels of pumps had to be used, in most cases, to bring water up to the surface. Some mines were lucky enough to have a stream nearby so its energy could be tapped by a water wheel. Most mines, however, depended on horse power to control the pumps. Large operations employed 50-60 horses 24 hours a day to turn the multiple pumps. Despite intense research from England's brightest minds, including the Royal Society of London, a true answer to mine drainage would not be found until the year 1712 when the precursor to the machine that would forever change the world first appeared in the small town of Dartmouth.

Fig. 14. Horse-Gin.

"The 17th Century (1603 to 1712)." 2012. The Rise of Coal in Britain. December 17. https://riseofcoalinbritain.wordpress.com/the-17th-century-1603-to-1712/.

While living in Littletown, at five years of age, I attended a one-room school with only one teacher for five, six, seven, and eight-year olds. We had one classroom with one teacher. The courtyard that we played in was divided with the boys on one side and the girls on the other.

Nine-year-olds went to Pittington School which was about a mile from Littletown. It was different at Pittington School. They taught us the normal things like reading, writing, and arithmetic, but they also taught us gardening, soccer, cricket, and sports. Each class had 40 to 45 students, as most of the teachers were called for war duty.

When we turned eleven, we took the Eleven Year Plus Exam. I didn't do very well on that exam, and that was fine with me, since I didn't like school anyway. I did not pass, and if you didn't pass that test, at fourteen years old, you were out of school.

These photos do not show all of Ron's brothers and sisters, but from top left, they are: Albert, Ann, William (Billy) with his son Freddy, and Frank at the microphone

The Kenney children (all but Doris). Clockwise from top left: Rose Kenney Cox with her husband Ken, Elizabeth Kenney Brunten, Ron with his old girlfriend Bea in 2006, Ron, Joseph, Joseph's wife Ethel, Albert, and Frank, and William with his wife Ethel.

Chapter 2—War Comes to England

Battle of Britain Banner featuring a British RAF Spitfire
made famous during the summer of 1940

When the war came to England in 1939, our house
still didn't have electricity.[3] There was gas, but we had
to pay for it. Having no electricity meant we didn't
have a radio, so we relied on the church bells to tell us
when to go to church or wherever. Our mother told
us one Sunday that we wouldn't be going to church
until that evening because England may be going to
war with Germany. She said if we heard the church
bell go "Dong, Dong, Dong!" it meant we were at

---

3   The Electricity Act of 1947 brought the distribution and supply ac-
     tivities of 505 separate organisations in England and Wales under
     state control and integrated them into 12 regional Area Boards.
     www.myutilitygenius.co.uk/guide/geeks/history-of-electricity/

war. Well, my brother and I took a walk to count our nest eggs,[4] and we heard the bell go "Dong, Dong, Dong!" It was about 11 o'clock in the morning, and we ran home. Mama was there crying, and she got all of us together and told us we were at war.

Mementos

I was eleven years old in 1940, and one day we were playing in the woods when we came upon a German hanging from a tree. We were scared to death. Our little group was made up of my brother and me and a few other boys. It was in a nice wooded place where we did most of our playing and that day the game was Cowboys and Indians.

We ran to the Home Guard[5] and told them what we had seen. We found out later that the man was dead, and we think to this day he was probably a spy. In our later years, my mother and I spoke about it. The officials gave each of us kids a piece of the parachute made of light green silk and a length

---

4 Ron and his brother Albert collected wild bird eggs. They would take one out of a nest and mark what kind of bird it was. Then they'd punch a small hole in the top and bottom and blow out the insides of the egg to keep them from smelling.

5 The Home Guard or Local Defence Volunteers (LDV) was a defensive arm of the British Army from 1940 to 1944. It was made up of 1.5 million volunteers otherwise ineligible for military service (i.e., too young or too old).
Macksey, Kenneth. *Beda Fomm: The Classic Victory.* New York: Ballantine, 1971..

of the rope from it. In those days, parachutes were pretty expensive, so that was a big deal.

Another time, we were playing football—what we call soccer over here in the US—when our headmaster, who served as coach and teacher because so many of the male teachers had gone into the service, blew his whistle and shouted for us to get in the ditch and lie flat. Then we heard an explosion in the next field. A German Messerschmitt had come down there. Some pieces of it landed on our football field, and we got to keep those.

The Messerschmitt 109 was Nazi Germany's primary fighter plane in the Battle of Britain. It was a worthy adversary to the Spitfire and Hurricane but had a major disadvantage, a limited range, so pilots could not stay long over Britain protecting their bombers.
(Trueman, C.N. "Messerschmitt 109." www.historylearningsite.co.uk.)

A few weeks later we found an incendiary bomb. It looked weird, so we didn't touch it—we'd been told not to touch anything, not even a pencil or a pen we might find, because they might be bombs. The Army came and took the detonator out of the bomb we found and just gave it to us! That was the funniest thing I'd ever heard of! They just gave it to us.

The parachute pieces, the incendiary bomb, and the German Messerschmitt fragments and are all in the Durham Museum today. My brother Albert and I donated them to the Pittington Museum, but they eventually gave them to the Durham Museum. My nephew Allen tried to locate them recently, and discovered that there were no names on anything and the donations from that time period were a jumbled up mess.

It was about six months later that Mother and all of us kids stood watching a dogfight up in the sky. A piece of shrapnel from a land mine about as big as a plate smashed through our house and split our back door, clean in half. We had no shelter to go to, so we all ran inside the house. Well, we thought no more about it and went to bed thinking the excitement was all over, but the next morning we got up and saw the fire department, the Home Guard, and the Army busy at work on the other side of our street. The Land mine actually struck the next street over. All the houses on that side of the street were flattened. There was nothing left except one second-story room. Even the stairway had crumbled. Our mother told us afterwards that there was a woman dead in that room, but her baby in a cradle beside her was still alive. There was

no roof left on the house, but there wasn't a speck
of dust on that baby's bed. So, miracles do happen.
One happened for that baby and for my whole family that night, while twenty-something other people

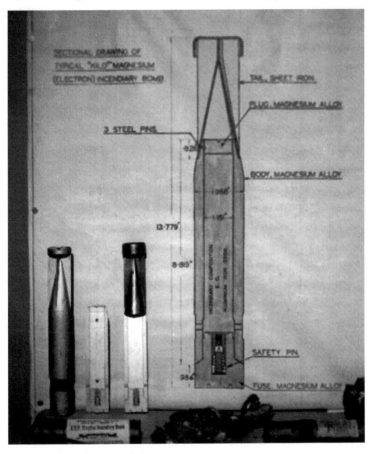

A training poster about the Brandbombe B1E. A one-kilo
bomb is shown, but there was also a two-kilo variety,
the B2E. These small incendiary bombs, which armed
as they fell, were among the most effective weapons
used against the UK in WWII. (http://ne-diary.genuki.uk/Bck/
BSeq_02.html#B11, Photo courtesy KGPA Ltd. / Alamy Stock Photo)

were killed right beside us.[6] When the war started, we were so far up north, that we didn't think the Germans would bother with us, but then later on we would stand outside and watch them dogfight over the skies and everything. We should've been scared but we weren't.

British police and Army bomb disposal officers with a defused 1000kg German Luftmine. These bombs were originally meant for use as sea mines. They were first used targets on land September 16, 1940. They were commonly referred to as "land mines."
(http://ne-diary.genuki.uk/Bck/BSeq_02.html#B11 photo from the Military History Collection / Alamy Stock Photo)

6   Ron adds that baby grew up to be an English footballer (a soccer player) who played for Sunderland United. There is a good description of incidents that took place from 29 August to 8 September, 1940 included in the Northeast Diary, 1939-1945 by Roy Ripley and Brian Pears. http://ne-diary.genuki.uk/Inc/ISeq_08.html#N364

Damage caused by Nazi air raids on the northeast
coast of England circa 1939-45.
(Trinity Mirror/ Mirrorpix/ Alamy Stock Photo)

After the Battle of Dunkirk, May 26 to June 4 of 1940, with all the British evacuated back to Britain from France, it looked pretty serious for England and Dad got us all together and I can remember to this day the words he said: "If Hitler gets within a hundred miles of where we are, I will throw you all into the Bricky Pond." It was a big pond and very deep. He meant to drown us all in there because he would not let the Germans have us. I believe he meant it too, because he would have gone with us. We didn't actually realize what he was talking about until after the war when we saw all the bad stuff in the newspapers about what the Nazis had done to other people in Europe. Then I could understand his reasoning.

At this point the Germans let up on us. They'd already taken France, and sent troops to Russia, then when Japan bombed Pearl Harbor, it brought the Americans to Europe to join the fight, and I believe that's what saved England.

Rationing

It was very different in England during the war to what it is now. Even though the newer houses in our village had electricity and running water installed inside by 1940,[7] we didn't even have hot water. We did have a single faucet in the house; it was by the side of the fireplace where we could fill the big cast iron pot. In the winter time, when the water was cut off because the pipes had frozen, we'd get snow, and put it in the pot to melt for our water. That was our drinking water, our washing water, everything. People today don't realize we were so primitive at that time. And the government would allow one egg a day for each of us. We had some chickens, but we had to keep a good count of the eggs. The rest of the eggs our family didn't eat would be picked up every three or four days.

We also had a hog, but if we killed it, half of that hog would have had to go to the government. It

---

7   This information about general conditions in the village comes from an online history of Dipton, "Walking in my Fore-father's Foot-steps" by Victor T.D. Holliday
http://www.durhamintime.org.uk/durham_miner/walking.pdf

didn't matter that we were a family of eleven. We got a fourth of a pound of sugar per week for the whole family. As the youngest child, I was lucky. When candy would come in, I was allowed to have my mother's and dad's portions. The officials would keep track of everything by looking at our ration books. They'd come to the house and check that we weren't cheating. They checked the chickens. If one died we had to tell them it died, and we weren't allowed to eat it. We had to show them the dead chicken.

People ask me how they had enough people to come around and check on everybody individually. Well, they were women and old men that couldn't go off to fight. There'd be one person come take care of this part, and another come take care of that part. So, one person wasn't responsible for checking on everything. And there was a night watchman who went around to check that no lights were showing at night.

It wasn't all bad. People helped each other out. In the row houses, the old people had a thick chain hanging down in their house, and in the bathrooms, and if they fell or got hurt they could pull that chain, and the nurse would come down and ask "What's up? Are you alright? Do you need help?" We never locked the door. And we used to have street parties—all getting together, in the street. And we walked or rode our bikes a lot more. If it was three miles to the shop, no one would bother to get the car out, even if they had one.

Chapter 3—Apprenticeship on Historic Grounds

Chastleton, Moreton-in-Marsh, Oxfordshire, England. Chastleton House is a historic Jacobean mansion, little altered from its original design. The Chastleton estate was once owned by Robert Catesby, one of the Gunpowder Plot instigators. That same family owned it for nearly 400 years until 1991. Originally built in 1603, the house has been restored and today it is cared for by the Brithsh National Trust.
(photo courtesy of Alamy)

The war was not over when I turned fourteen and finished school. I needed a job, so my father, naturally, took me to the coal mine to get me signed on there, but the foreman told my dad that they couldn't find a job for a boy who only weighed 58 pounds. My older brothers had gone to work in the mine at the same age, and my sisters had been sent to London to work as maids in rich people's houses.

Well, in the next town over there was a bookie, and when my dad bet there, he was known as Pigeon Joe because he used to raise and race pigeons. He won a lot of trophies doing that. This bookie, George Fevell, got me a job with a race horse trainer, Mr. Drinkwater, and my Dad put me on a train from Durham and pinned a tag to my coat that had my name and Mr. Drinkwater's name and address printed on it.

It was about 400 miles from home. My mother gave me a jam sandwich and a shilling (about 25 cents) so I could get something to eat and drink on my way. When we had to change trains, the porter got me on the right train, and when I got to Moreton-in-Marsh that was the end of the train ride. Mr. Drinkwater was there to pick me up. I had my bicycle with me, but he told me to leave it at the station and we would get it the next day. When I got to Chastleton House Stables, he had a cot set up for me in the tack room (a tack room is where they keep saddles and bridles). His wife gave me a glass of milk and some cookies for my supper. That tack room was my home for the next three months, at which point I ran away, trying to get home. I got as far as the Oxford train station when the police found me and took me back.

That is when Mr. Drinkwater found me a place with a family. Though Drinkwater only had 5 to 10 horses at any one time, it took three of us to look after them. I was very, very lucky, because Mr. Drinkwater's wasn't a very big stable, so lodgings were arranged for me with Mr. and Mrs. Bert Smith and their family. I lived with them for sixteen years, until I came to this country in 1960. They were wonderful people, and they more or less raised me. Mr. and Mrs. Smith have since died, but I still go back to England and stay with their daughter, Doreen, and her husband. Doreen was nine years old when I went to live with them.

For a few years while I was there I dated a girl called Beatrice Hunt. I met her at a dance, and she lived on her daddy's farm a couple of farms over. I would have married her, but my apprenticeship agreement specified that I could not marry until the term was up. She married my friend, and they started a family. Later, after I couldn't ride anymore, I used to take Bea on the back of my motorcycle dancing, while he stayed home with the kids! I lost contact with Beatrice for years until after my wife passed away and I went back to England for a visit. In recent years, I've lost contact with her again.

Clockwise from top left: Mrs. Smith with her family, Mrs. Smith with her dog, Mrs. Heath's daughter, Mr. and Mrs. Bert Smith, a motorcycle similar to Ron's BSA M20, and Mrs. Smith's father, a farmer, who lived with us for a while.

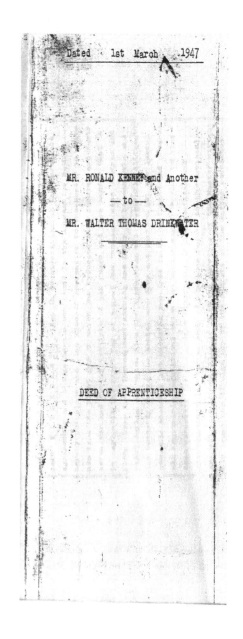

Dated   1st March   1947

MR. RONALD KENNEY and Another

— to —

MR. WALTER THOMAS DRINKWATER

DEED OF APPRENTICESHIP

26

T H I S   A P P R E N T I C E S H I P   D E E D made the First
day of March One thousand nine hundred and forty seven BETWEEN——
RONALD KENNEY of Chastleton House Stables Moreton-in-Marsh in the
County of Gloucester (hereinafter called "the Apprentice") of the
first part JOSEPH HALL KENNEY of 9 Front Street Little Town Durham
in the County of Durham the father of the Apprentice (hereinafter
called "the Guardian") of the second part and WALTER THOMAS ————
DRINKWATER of Chastleton House Stables Moreton-in-Marsh aforesaid
Trainer of Horses (hereinafter called "the Master") of the third——
part W I T N E S S E T H that in consideration of the covenants
agreements and things herein contained He the Apprentice doth ——
hereby put place and bind himself Apprentice to the Master to serve
him from the First day of March One thousand nine hundred and forty
seven for and during the term of six years and five months that is
to say until the First day of August One thousand nine hundred and
fifty three from thence next ensuing and fully to be complete and
ended during all which time the Apprentice will faithfully diligently
and honestly serve the Master and obey and perform all his lawful
commands whenever and wherever required to be performed and observe
all reasonable regulations which the Master may from time to time
deem necessary for the proper discipline of his business and ——
establishment (so far as such regulations relate to Apprentices)——
And will not absent himself from the services of the Master without
his leave nor divulge any of the secrets of the Master connected——
with his business or otherwise but will keep and preserve the same
and will not unduly or negligently spend or waste any of the moneys
effects goods or chattels of the Master which shall at any time be
entrusted or placed in his hands or custody either by the Master or
by any other person or persons on his account during the said term
And will well and truly from time to time account for deliver or——
pay to the Master his executors administrators or assigns all such
moneys and other things as the Apprentice shall receive have or be
entrusted with or which shall come to his hands or possession for
or on account of the Master or for or on account of the services of
or work done by the Apprentice during the said term And Also will
in all matters and things whatsoever during the said term demean——

27

and behave himself as a good true and faithful Apprentice ought to——
do And the Master doth hereby covenant with the Apprentice and with
the Guardian in manner following that is to say That he the Master——
will at the request of the Apprentice and with such consent as———
aforesaid take and receive the Apprentice for and during the said———
term And Also will during the said term (Provided always that and——
only so long as the Apprentice performs and observes all the promises
matters and things hereinbefore contained to be performed and———
observed on his part) to the best of his power knowledge and ability
teach and instruct the Apprentice in the arts of a Training Groom——
which he useth and of riding as connected therewith and find and——
provide for him the Apprentice good proper and sufficient meat drink
and lodging And Also will subject to the same proviso pay or allow
to the Apprentice as and by way of wages during the said term after
the rates following that is to say the sum of Twenty five pounds——
during the first year thereof the sum of Thirty pounds during the——
second year thereof the sum of Thirty five pounds during the third—
year thereof the sum of Forty pounds during the fourth year thereof
the sum of Forty five pounds during the fifth year thereof the sum—
of Fifty pounds during the sixth year thereof and after the rate of
Fifty five pounds per annum during the last five months thereof And
Also will pay or allow to the Apprentice one half of any moneys which
shall be received by the Master or the Apprentice for presents or——
riding fees in consequence of the work done by the Apprentice during
the whole of the said term after deducting a proportionate share of
the expenses (if any) that may be incurred in earning and collecting
the same And the Guardian doth hereby covenant and agree with the——
Master that the Apprentice shall and will faithfully diligently and
honestly serve the Master as his Apprentice during the said term and
according to the true intent and meaning of these presents and will
perform and observe all the promises matters and things hereinbefore
contained to be performed and observed by the Apprentice and that in
default thereof either wholly or in part the Guardian shall and will
pay to the Master the sum of Five pounds to be recovered as and by
way of liquidated or ascertained damages And Further that the———

28

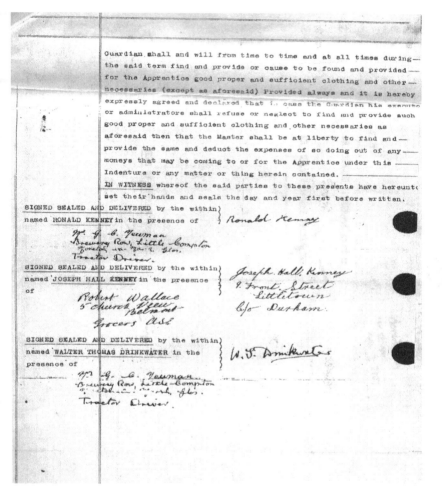

Guardian shall and will from time to time and at all times during—
the said term find and provide or cause to be found and provided—
for the Apprentice good proper and sufficient clothing and other—
necessaries (except as aforesaid) Provided always and it is hereby
expressly agreed and declared that in case the Guardian his executors
or administrators shall refuse or neglect to find and provide such
good proper and sufficient clothing and other necessaries as
aforesaid then that the Master shall be at liberty to find and—
provide the same and deduct the expenses of so doing out of any—
moneys that may be coming to or for the Apprentice under this—
Indenture or any matter or thing herein contained.—
IN WITNESS whereof the said parties to these presents have hereunto
set their hands and seals the day and year first before written.

SIGNED SEALED AND DELIVERED by the within⎫
named RONALD KENNEY in the presence of ⎬ *Ronald Kenney*

Mr G. C. Yeuman
Brewery Row, Little Compton
——— in May & Glos.
Tractor Driver.

SIGNED SEALED AND DELIVERED by the within⎫
named JOSEPH HALL KENNEY in the presence ⎬ *Joseph Hall Kenney*
of   ⎭ *9. Front Street*
                                             Littletown
Robert Wallace   *c/o Durham.*
5 Church View
Belmont
Grocers Ass?

SIGNED SEALED AND DELIVERED by the within⎫
named WALTER THOMAS DRINKWATER in the   ⎬ *W. T. Drinkwater*
presence of

Mr G. C. Yeuman
Brewery Row, Little Compton
——— Station in May & Glos.
Tractor Driver.

Ron's Deed of Apprenticeship with Mr. Walter Thomas
Drinkwater. Ron's father was paid £50 (fifty pounds
sterling) when Ron finally signed these papers.
These apprenticeship papers and the ones that follow
are on display in the Hitchcock Museum in
Hitchcock, Texas.

I did not sign my apprenticeship papers with Mr. Drinkwater until I was nearly seventeen years old. I didn't have a real reason not to sign, but someone told me not to sign them, so I didn't want to do it. It was just something that got stuck in my mind. I was just a kid; I wasn't supposed to know anything. My dad eventually convinced me to sign the apprenticeship papers for six years and so many months—agreeing to serve until I was 23 years old. I learned later that when I finally signed, Mr. Drinkwater paid my dad £50, the equivalent of $202.00 US.[8] To be an apprentice, then, meant that I agreed to serve my master and nobody else, with everything.

I served with Mr. Drinkwater for a while. He made me big promises, but he actually gave me nothing. He promised me I could ride in races, but I never did. I had not been home to see my mother for more than three years. But by that time, though, Mr. Drinkwater was leaving Chastleton Stables to go to some other place. He had changed from training race horses to training hunting horses, and it was a good thing for me, because he sold my contract to Mr. Heath when I was about 17 years old.

I never really knew what happened, but all of a sudden one day, I was told that Mr. Heath would

---

8   From 1940, and through the war, the £/$ rate was pegged by the British government at $4.03, and at the end of the war a world conference in Bretton Woods, New Hampshire, decided on a variation of the Gold Standard, which Britain adopted in December 1945, maintaining the pound at $4.03. In effect, the Americans sowed the seeds for one of Britain's biggest financial crises. http://www.miketodd.net/encyc/dollhist-graph.htm

be coming in two or three days and he would be my new boss. I was thankful when Drinkwater left Chastleton House Stables and Mr. Heath took over. The period that followed was one of the most wonderful parts of my life because Mr. Heath was a good man. He was one of the best people in the world. He treated me like I was a normal person. I not only worked for Mr. Heath, I became friends with his daughter, Lynn. She was four years old when I first knew her.

Chastleton House stable yard today.
(photo courtesy of Alamy)

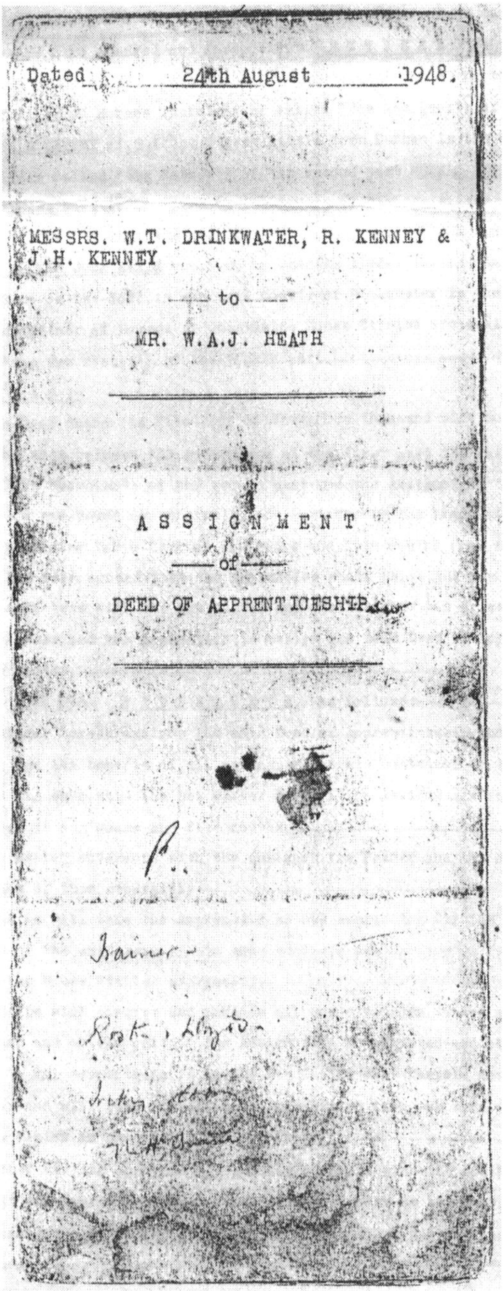

Dated   24th August   1948.

MESSRS. W.T. DRINKWATER, R. KENNEY &
J.H. KENNEY

to

MR. W.A.J. HEATH

A S S I G N M E N T

of

DEED OF APPRENTICESHIP

This ASSIGNMENT is made the Twenty fourth day of August One thousand nine hundred and forty eight B E T W E E N WALTER THOMAS DRINKWATER of Shipton Court Stables Shipton-under-Wychwood in the County of Oxford Trainer of Horses (hereinafter called "the Assignor") of the first part JOSEPH HALL KENNEY of 9 Front Street Little Town Durham in the County of Durham (hereinafter called "the Father") of the second part RONALD KENNEY of Chastleton House Stables Moreton-in-Marsh in the County of Gloucester the son of the said Joseph Hall Kenney (hereinafter called "the Apprentice") of the third part and WILFRED ARCHER JOHN HEATH employed by Charles Albert Joseph Scarrott of Central Garage Stow-on-the-Wold in the said County of Gloucester in the business of Licensed Trainer of Horses at Chastleton House Stables aforesaid (hereinafter called "the New Master") of the fourth part.

W H E R E A S :-

(1) By a Deed dated the First day of March One thousand nine hundred and forty seven and made between the Apprentice of the first part the Father (thereinafter called "the Guardian") of the second part and the Assignor of the third part the Apprentice was bound Apprentice to the Assignor in the trade of Training Groom and Horse Riding for a term of six years and five months from the date thereof.

(2) It has been agreed that the Apprentice shall serve the now unexpired residue of the said term with the New Master and the Assignor has agreed with the consent of the Father and the Apprentice to assign the said Deed of Apprenticeship to the New Master.

N O W   T H I S   D E E D   W I T N E S S E T H   as follows:-

1.   The Assignor hereby assigns the said Deed of Apprenticeship and all his interest therein and the benefit of all covenants therein contained to the New Master TO HOLD the same unto the New Master for all the residue now unexpired of the said term of six years and five months.

2.   The New Master covenants with the Assignor the Father and the Apprentice and with each of them separately:-

(a) That he will take the Apprentice as his Apprentice for the now unexpired residue of the said term in his said business now carried on by him at Chastleton House Stables aforesaid;

(b) That he will observe and perform all the covenants in the said Deed contained and on the part of the Assignor to be observed and performed in like manner in all respects as if he the New Master were therein named instead of the Assignor and will keep the Assignor indemnified from the same and from all actions claims or demands in respect thereof.

3.   The Father and the Apprentice severally covenant with the New Master:-

(a) That the Apprentice shall serve the New Master as his Apprentice in his said business now carried on by him at Chastleton House Stables aforesaid for

THIS IS TO CERTIFY that the within-named RONALD KENNEY has duly served his period of apprenticeship as laid down by the Apprenticeship Deed herein recited dated the First day of March One thousand nine hundred and forty seven to the complete satisfaction in all respects of myself the within-named WILFRED ARCHER JOHN HEATH so far as concerns the period of the within written Deed of Assignment.

Dated this First day of August One thousand nine hundred and fifty three.

Signed :- *WHeath*

---

all the residue now unexpired of the said term;

(b) That they and each of them will observe and perform all the covenants in the said deed contained and on their part to be observed and performed in like manner in all respects as if the New Master were therein named instead the Assignor.

IN WITNESS whereof the said parties hereto have hereunto set their hands and seals the day and year first before written.

SIGNED SEALED AND DELIVERED by the said)
WALTER THOMAS DRINKWATER in the
presence of
C. Seasson
Central garage
Stow on the Wold

Walter Thomas Drinkwater

SIGNED SEALED AND DELIVERED by the said)
JOSEPH HALL KENNEY in the presence of)
George Favell.
Crispin Arms. Sherburn Hill
Co. Durham.
Public House Manager.

Joseph Hall Kenney.

SIGNED SEALED AND DELIVERED by the said)
RONALD KENNEY in the presence of)
Mr George, Newman.

Ronald Kenney

When Walter Thomas Drinkwater left the stables at Chastleton House, Ron's apprentice papers were signed over to Mr. Wilford Archer John Heath. Ron refers to this as one of the best things that happened in his life.

At Right: Top: A very young Lynn Heath, and Bottom: Ron and Lynn Heath on Lynn's pony some years later.

Mr. Heath allowed me to start riding in races as an apprentice. As Mr. Heath was the owner of my contract, he received half of all the money I made over my weekly income. However, the day I finished my apprenticeship, he gave every penny back to me. That is how I was able to come to America. Mr. Heath gave me some rides in races where I did very well, so he had saved up a nice sum for me.

I was like a rich kid when I was with Mr. Heath, because I owned a motorcycle. The rest of the kids around there had to walk unless they had a bicycle. In fact, at Chastleton House, there weren't even that many cars: Mr. Heath had a car, there was a car for the staff at the big house, Mr. Townsend, the farmer, had a car, and Peter Walwyn's Dad, Taffy Walwyn[9] had a car, and that was it. Four cars among a hundred and fifty or so families living there.

I won the motorcycle in my first race. It was at Chepstow on a horse owned by Mr. Scarrett. I was just over sixteen years of age. Mr. Heath said, "it's a six-furlong race on a horse called Davina." He told me to sit somewhere around third or sixth place until I was an eighth of a mile from the finish line. He said, "hold her back, but when you come up on that crest of the hill," (the race track was uphill until the last 100 yards and it was all downhill on the back side), "then let her go. You'll win easy, but I don't want you to win by too much." That was because he didn't want everyone to know how fast the horse really was. He didn't want to tip the bookies off. But she was a fine little mare, and when the tape went up (no starting gates back then), I jumped out in front, and won by six lengths. When I got to the winner's circle, I could tell Mr. Heath was not pleased, then I knew I had not ridden to order, but the owner of

9   Major "Taffy" Walwyn was the father of Peter Walwyn, who became one of England's foremost racehorse trainers from the 1960s. He was just starting to train horses when Ron left England. He learned a great deal from Mr. Heath.

the horse, Mr. Scarrett, was pleased. He said, "I'll tell you what I'll do; I'll give you ten percent of my winnings, or I'll give you a motorcycle, because I own a motorcycle business." I took the motorcycle (a BSA 450). I'd have had to share the money with my boss, but I could keep the entire motorcycle. And I did keep that motorcycle until I gave it away when I came to this country in 1960. (There is a picture of a bike like mine at the bottom of page 25.)

I had a few winners with Mr. Heath as he only had a small stable, but my weight—75-80 lbs.—got me a lot of rides from other trainers. I rode some for Major Cunard, owner of the Queen Mary cruise ship among others. The most exciting one was when Mr. Heath called and told me I was going to Paris, France to ride in the French Gold Cup for an Arabian Prince. The horse was called Black Tarquen. We did not win the race, but I did finish 3rd out of a field of 28 horses, some from England and other countries. After so many wins as an apprentice, I lost some of my weight allowance (apprentice jockeys were given 7 lbs. off the weight they had to carry in the race) so if he had to carry say 100 lbs. the horse would carry 93 lbs. with the apprentice allowance. At 19 I was cut down to only 3 lbs. allowance because I had won so many races. I was never given a picture that showed me winning a race.

That is when I started drinking heavy. I had money and you couldn't tell me anything. I knew it all, so I thought. Even Mr. Heath was not giving me rides in the races. By the time I reached 23 I may have gotten one ride in a race per month. I think the good Lord took over my life at that point. I got rheumatic fever and was in the hospital for three months and another three months in a convalescence home. While I was there, Mr. Heath still paid Mrs. Smith for my room and paid me my wages, but he said that when I got out, if I had not stopped drinking, when my apprenticeship was over he was going to let me go. Mrs. Smith said the same thing. They had all they could take of my drinking. Well, the first thing I did after getting out of the convalescence home was go to the beer joint for a beer. It tasted terrible, and I have not drunk a beer since then. I still say God saved me.

I was not allowed to ride races anymore, but Mr. Heath kept me on and started teaching me how to train horses and get them ready to race and everything he knew about horses, so I stayed with him until I was 30 years old and came to the States. When I left, he told me I had a job if I ever came back to England.

Mr. Heath, Lynn, and Ron on a visit in 2002.

Chapter 4—Odd Jobs

The only time the horses were ever moved out of the stables at Chastleton House was when the American Army stopped there while they were getting ready for D-Day. (Of course this happened years before I was there.) The dividers for the horse stalls and everything were taken out, and they used the space as the mess hall. After it was all over, the Americans restored everything and put the stalls back. The bars on the stalls were brass, so my boss put black paint

over them so we wouldn't have to worry about any-
one trying to steal them.

The Americans had hooked up electricity to
the whole place. The stables and the barn and everything around were wired up with 110-volt electricity.[10] When I left in 1960, we were still using the
same generator with batteries. The big house still
does not have electricity. Today it is a museum and
they make movies there. The village itself didn't get
electricity until 1953, but the oldest parts of the village still don't have electricity—the ones with the
thatched roofs.

**Lynn Heath ready for the hunt at the gates of
Chastleton House.** (Photo from Ron Kenney's personal library)

---

10 Normally electricity in England is 220 volt, but the American troops
wired the stable up with 110 volt.

My day-to-day work wasn't always about riding race horses. One example was Major Cunard. He kept three horses with us for many years. One was a race horse, but the other two were hunting horses. Well, Major Cunard used to come down during hunting season—on Saturdays—in his old-fashioned Rolls Royce. He would be there by 6 o'clock in the morning after driving all the way from London, and he would take one horse out on the hunt. Then, 'round about dinner time, I'd have to set the next horse out to meet him and then bring the dirty horse back and clean it up—wash it and clean the tack and everything. He'd get back in with the second horse sometimes later than 7 o'clock in the evening and I'd have to stay there and clean that horse up too. I sometimes didn't finish until 9 o'clock or later at night, so it was a pretty long day for me, but he always gave me a shilling. A shilling may not seem like much, but at the time, I was only making 2 and 6 pence a week for pocket money.[11]

I used to do some part-time work in the garden and around the place to earn some extra money. One day, Mrs. Whitmore-Jones, wife of the owner, asked us to go down to the dungeons and see what was down there and clean up a bit. It hadn't been cleaned up in who-knows-how-many years. Well, we went

---

11 A shilling is worth one twentieth of a pound sterling, or twelve pence. In other words, there were 240 pence to one pound sterling. In 1947, 2 and 6 pence equaled approximately $2.66 US, but accounting for inflation, that $2.66 is now equal to $29.42! http://www.in2013dollars.com/1947-dollars-in-2018?amount=2.66

down there and we found one of the pewter dinner sets, and it was the only complete pewter set remaining. It is now on display in the Oxford Museum.

A view of the church across the clipped yew circle at Chastleton House.
(The National Trust Photolibrary / Alamy Stock Photo)

Barbara Hayes and Ron standing in front of part of a pewter dinner set at Chastelton House in 2006. This is not the same set Ron found in the dungeon.

Another little job of mine was helping with the organ on Sundays. St Mary's Church, Chastleton, first built in AD 1100, is still standing, and they still hold services there. When I lived at Chastleton, the church had a pump organ. They still play that same organ today, but they've electrified it now, and it doesn't have to be powered with a bellows. Back in 1952, at 11 o'clock in the morning on Sunday, I was to go down there and pump that organ by hand for Mrs. Whitmore-Jones who was still alive and going strong. She played the organ, while I lay underneath working the bellows, and if I'd go too slow, she'd kick me under the seat to get me to pump the organ faster.

Allen Hayes and Ron standing beside a tomb from the 1600s on a visit to Chastleton House in 2006.

Chastleton House has a strong connection to the Guy Fawkes celebration that takes place every year in England. Not a lot of people in America actually learn much about English history, so it's worth explaining that in 1605, Robert Catesby, a former owner of Chastleton House, was the main instigator behind a plot to blow up the Houses of Parliament. History classes teach it as "The Gunpowder Plot." A man named Guy Fawkes was caught with barrels of gunpowder, and his name is the one everyone remembers, but it was Catesby who actually led the plot. Catesby had been forced to sell Chastleton House and his lands to pay fines following his imprisonment for his participation in the earlier 1601 Essex Rebellion. However, his mother still lived in Chastleton House. It is believed that Catesby and his fellow conspirators spent time in Chastleton House in 1605 prior to the events commemorated by the burning of the Guy Fawkes effigy on the fourth of November each year.

The story I was told when I worked there is that the men who cooked up the Gunpowder Plot escaped to Chastleton House when they were trying to get away from Cromwell's men, hid in a priest hole,[12] and escaped when a sympathetic maid got Cromwell's men so drunk they fell asleep. It turns

12 Hiding places or "priest's holes" were built in these houses in case there was a raid. Priest holes were built in fireplaces, attics and staircases and were largely constructed between the 1550s and the Catholic-led Gunpowder Plot in 1605. Sometimes other building alterations would be made at the same time as the priest's holes so as not to arouse suspicion. http://www.historic-uk.com/HistoryUK/HistoryofEngland/Priests-Holes/

out, I got the historical characters confused. It was a different man, named Arthur Jones, whose grandfather bought the place from Catesby, who hid out in the secret room, or priest hole, following the Battle of Worcester. The Roundhead soldiers followed him, and Arthur's wife, Sarah, drugged the soldiers and helped her husband to escape.

I had friends at the Chastleton House Stables. One of these was Tim Farnsworth, who later became a prominent conservative member of the House of Commons in the British Parliament. Tim came to work with us briefly as a teenager because he wanted to learn how to ride. He rode one race for us and won it.

Ron at 25 years of age on a horse called Mountain Earl,
a big three-mile steeple chaser.

Ron rarely saw his parents during his apprenticeship. These pictures show some of those rare visits and offer a glimpse of Ron's gregarious nature as he makes a funny face over his parents' shoulders and jokes with a friend. Clockwise from top left: Ron's father in 1950, his father and mother, Ron clowning around with Tim Farnsworth, Mr. and Mrs. Kenney with Ron, and Ron pulling a face over his parents' shoulders.

Chapter 5—Welcome to Texas

I never intended to stay in America. I only meant to work here for a year or two. My sister Doris had married an American GI from Fort Worth while the war was on, and when she came home to visit in 1960, she said to me, "Why don't you come back with me to America and I'll get you a job throwing papers. You'll make more money there than you do here."

I said, "Well, I've got enough English money saved for two or three years, then I'll come back to England."

When I got off the plane at Fort Worth, I thought I was going to die. I had on a double breasted tweed suit and a tie and it was about a hundred degrees outside. I had never been anyplace that hot. In those days, airports were not air conditioned, and neither were the cars.

I was broke within a few weeks. As an immigrant, I was supposed to go to the employment office to sign up for jobs and take any job that was offered to me, so I went down there to sign up for a job. They gave me a form to fill out, but the girl at the desk had to help fill it out as my education was not very good. I could not spell or read very well. My sister dropped me off but told me to get the bus back to her house, since she had to pick her daughter up from school.

There was a saddle shop right there in downtown Fort Worth where I was waiting for the bus. I met the owner of the saddle shop, Arthur Tiner. He asked me if I was looking for a job, and he said, "Give me some change and I'll call down to this man and see if he wants to hire you." So, I let him call and I talked to Mr. Tommy Oliphant.[13]

---

13 Oliver "Tommy" Oliphant, of Sabinal, Texas, trained race horses for nearly six decades. In 1959 he built Sunny Clime Farms, in partnership with Dr. Dan Saunders. He was honored among Texas race horse trainers with numerous awards including being inducted into the Texas Horse Racing Hall of Fame. http://americanracehorse.com/tommy-oliphant-member-of-texas-horse-racing-hall-of-fame-dies-at-88/

Mr. Oliphant said, "Come on down." It was in Sabinal, Texas. So, three days later I was on my way down to Tommy Oliphant's and I stayed with him for a while.

The first morning on my new job, they tried to make sure that I could ride. The horse was only half broke, so when I got on the track it started bucking and went down on its knees. I knew everyone there was having a great time at my expense, but when I came back up still on the horse's back, they all started clapping, so I got the job. Tommy Oliphant was really good to me, and they had a cook who could do most anything with eggs and deer meat. That was our main meal—that and biscuits with black molasses. It sure was good.

One day, this pickup truck and a two-horse trailer pulled up with a man, a young woman and a baby (I believe the baby was Kim). The young woman was about 20 or 21 years old. The man was this big Texas-looking man who introduced himself and his wife to Mr. Oliphant. I think Tommy already knew who they were. He turned around and introduced them to me: Buster and Pat Parish. They had a young horse they wanted someone to break. It was a Quarter Horse, and nobody there wanted a Quarter Horse to break, but I said, "I'll take it." The mare, Bo's Hope, didn't need breaking because she was so gentle and quiet and spoiled. I had no idea those people would be part of my life from that day on.

Clockwise from top left: The Parish truck and trailer, Buster and Pat Parish, and a filly named Bo's Hope with Buster Parish.

Learning to Drive

In the meantime, my brother-in-law Leroy sold me a 1950 Ford Custom for $50. He even brought it all the way from Fort Worth to Sabinal, as I didn't know how to drive a car yet. I drove around the farm and the back streets with the help of Sonny Crowl, another jockey who worked for Tommy Oliphant. One weekend while we were there, Dr. Dan Saunders' two boys asked if they could borrow the car because I hadn't gotten my driver's license yet. I didn't tell them no because Dr. Saunders was the owner of the place. They said they wanted to see if I liked their car, a 1957 Chevrolet, and maybe we'd make a deal on Monday or something.

I said, "Okay, I'll see what I can do."

They took my car off somewhere over the weekend and sold it. They came back to me on Monday and asked for my papers so they could get the deal done.

I said, "No, I want to keep my car." I had never agreed to let them sell my car.

A 1950 Ford Custom.

Well, there were a few words spoken, and Dr. Saunders invited me to his house and told me what he'd heard about it.

I told him, "No, I want to keep my car."

He said, "You know, in Texas when we do a handshake," he said, "we believe it."

I said, "I never shook hands on it," I said. "And I'm not from Mexico, I'm from England. I may have come from over water, but I am still the owner of my car, and that's what I want." I told him I was going to call the police. Well, the week before I had gone down and taken my written driving test, and I'd passed it, but I was waiting for somebody to take me into town to do the driving test behind the wheel.

Dr. Saunders said, "You can have the car, but I think you'd better leave." I believe he had to buy my car back from whoever his boys had sold it to for more money than they got for it. He was really the big boss, though Tommy Oliphant was the trainer, Saunders owned the place, so I had to leave.

I said, "Okay, I will." I went straight to the police station and told them my situation. The police gave me a piece of paper to carry with me that said I'd passed my driver's test, and they gave me a map to Fort Worth to my sister's house. They wouldn't give you a piece of paper like that nowadays.

Chapter 6—Pat and Buster Parish

Pat and Buster Parish in about 1962

When I got to my sister's house, there was a phone message waiting for me from Pat and Buster Parish. They wanted me to come to work for them.

I said, "Okay."

It was in Houston, so they said I could live in the house at their stable on Brittmoore Road if I wanted to. At first I stayed with Buster's parents.

Buster and Pat were opening up a saddle shop, called Salt Grass Saddlery. So, I went to Houston in my 1950 Ford Custom and worked for them for a while. That was the start of a long friendship.

Pat (Parish) Cole's Recollections of Ron Kenney

Written: July 22, 2017

A lot of things happened in my life in 1960 and 1961. I married Buster Parish from Houston, Texas, moved to his ranch in Junction, Texas, and had a precious little girl born prematurely. Kim weighed 2 pounds and 15 ounces.

About the same time, a Thoroughbred mare that Cliney Cochcran had given to Buster had a filly by Hobo Adam, a Quarter Horse stallion that Buster had gotten from B. L. Smith. I fell in love with the black, blue eyed, stocking-legged little wild child of a filly. I was the only one who could put a hand on her. I named her "Bo's Hope."

In the spring of 1961, Junction had a big goat sale and several days of horse racing. We decided to take Bo down to a horse trainer in Sabinal to get her trained for that race. I had been riding her snubbed up by one of our hombres to my horse, King Joe Doc.

We put her in the trailer and began our trip to the track with our first race horse. After arriving, we met the head honcho who turned us over to an Englishman named Ron Kenney. I gave Ron all sorts of instructions for Hope's care and treatment,

---

such as being sure to scratch the top of her tail when she backed up to him. I didn't want him to think she was going to kick him.

After we left the track and Sabinal that day I worried that they, the experts, would not know how to take care of my spoiled little darling. Early the next day, I was on the phone to the trainer to check on her and was connected with Ron. He was very nice, obviously recognizing me as a real amateur. He told me that the farrier had put shoes on her front feet the day before, but she had gotten them off before the sun came up. Of course, that wasn't true, but I believed everything he told me.

As the month progressed, we went down to see the filly work and got to know Ron better and really liked him a lot. There was a vet who owned the property and he had two sons. It appeared those boys were trying to cheat Ron over a car deal, and right in the middle of Bo's training, Ron was having to leave, so we hired him to come work for us.

For a brief time, Ron moved to Junction and our ranch on the South Llano River and helped us gather stock to sell for our move back to Houston. He was out in the brush and rattlesnakes on a two-year-old, barely broke young stallion in a forward seat, jumping saddle. What a hoot that was! I'll never understand how an Englishman spoke Spanish well enough to work all day with our Mexican "wet backs."

One day when we were gathering stock nine miles back in the ranch. Buster's daughters Penny and Pam, and my little sister, Judy, were there at the ranch. They were all in their early teens, riding and generally getting in the middle of everything. Ron had been keeping an eye on them while Buster and I took baby Kim back to the house as the day was ending.

Ron and the girls were at the pens in the back in an old blue Chevy pickup we had, and sometime shortly after dark, they started back toward the house. After they went through a gate, the truck died and rolled back against the gate and refused to start again. Of course this was way before cell phones, and Ron had no way of getting word to us at the house where I was dithering and worrying about what what was taking them so long. Buster had already gone to bed. Finally around 1:00 a.m., I got in the station wagon dressed in my flannel "granny" nightgown and went to the back ranch looking for them.

There they were. Ron had the girls all in the back of that old truck covered up with feed sacks to keep them warm. I took them all home, fed them and put them to bed.

And that is the first story that comes to mind when any member of our family speaks of Ron Kenney, even to this day. Of course, it is not the only story!

Chapter 7—The Mecom Years

John W. Mecom
(photo by Donald Uhrbrock The LIFE Images Collection/ Getty Images.)

One day while I was helping out at Salt Grass Saddlery, a veterinarian by the name of Doc Williams asked me if I would go down to Hitchcock, Texas, and help him with an operation on a polo pony that belonged to John W. Mecom. The horse's nasal membranes had stopped up, and he needed a tracheotomy. The vet had never done one before, but I had seen three of those operations done before.

I said, "Who's Mecom?"[14]

Williams said, "He's just a millionaire. I'll pick you up and we'll fly down there." And that's how we went—by plane—to meet Mr. Mecom. After the surgery on the horse, Mr. Mecom asked me if I would like to go to work for him. He told me that he was building a race track, and he was going to put most of his race horses there. He said he wanted me to be his trainer.

I said, "Oh!" That was a big deal for me, and what I really wanted to do, because Buster and Pat Parish didn't have any race horses most of the time. They had pleasure horses and cutting horses and stuff like that. It was all right but it was not my real line.

After paying what I owed Buster, I moved to Hitchcock to start work at the Mecom Ranch. I had exactly $7.11 in my pocket, and I wasn't going to get paid for three weeks.

I said, "Whoa! What am I going to do? What can I do with $7.11 for three weeks?" There was a little café called Jack Frost and it was owned by two

14 John Whitfield Mecom, Sr. was a famous Houston oilman who ranked with J. Paul Getty and H. L. Hunt as one of the world's wealthiest men. His ability to produce and supply petroleum during WWII won this position for him. Mecom experienced some spectacular failures as well as spectacular successes, as do most very wealthy people. www.nytimes.com/1981/10/14/obituaries/john-w-mecom-sr-is-dead-at-70-texan-was-giant-among-oilmen.html

ladies called the Turners, so I went in there, and me being a bold and desperate Englishman, I told them, "Look, I've come to work for Mecom, but I don't have any money. Still, I'd like to have a place to eat until I get paid in three weeks."

They were very kind, and they said, "We'll give you a tab and let you eat here. Big meal for dinner, we don't open on Sundays but we'll let you eat for three weeks here. But you better pay up when the time comes."

I said, "I sure will and I appreciate it." And I still appreciate those people.

There was a lady who lived on the land where the old blimp base had been during WWII. She was called Mrs. Domain, and she knew my situation, because every Sunday for the next eight or nine weeks she'd bring me my dinner. I appreciated that. At Schanzer's grocery store at the time you could buy six cans of Heinz soup for a dollar, especially the ones that had a dent in them. Saltine crackers were 17 cents for a package. That was my breakfast and supper for the next three weeks, which is why today, I still don't like Heinz soup or crackers very much. I believe that God was with me all that time, and that He still is.

A Blind Date

Doubling back to 1962, I was buying my gas and everything from a Texaco station in Hitchcock, which was owned by Charlie Brundrett. His wife Nell was president at the bank in Hitchcock. One day I was there buying gas when he said, "Hey, would you like to go to a party?"

I said, "Okay."

He said, "Bring your girlfriend."

I said, "I don't have one."

He said, "Well, I'll try and find you one."

So, I got to the party and there was this woman doing the twist with a towel. I said "Whoa! What kind of party is this?" I found out right away that the woman with the towel was my date. I discovered later that she was also a lot of fun. When I started to take her home, we stopped, and I said, "Can I see you again?"

She said, "Well, if you knew how many kids I've got you wouldn't want to see me again."

I said, "I don't care how many kids you've got," and we dated for quite a while. I learned that she had four children; all girls, and that she'd had a pretty rough life with it.

Seven months later, I married Patsy Hepler Hamrick on July 12, 1963 at Patsy's parents' house. It was on a Friday evening and we were on our honeymoon until Sunday evening. We went to San Antonio and down to Sabinal to see Tommy Oliphant. I went back at work on Monday. We had to honeymoon on her paycheck.

Patsy Hepler Hamrick (pictured) and Ron Kenney were married July 12, 1963. They were married for almost 43 years. Patsy passed away March 31, 2006.

At the time I met Patsy, she worked for the Hitchcock water department. She did just about everything there. Later on in our marriage she voluneered at the library for our local Catholic Church, Our Lady Of Lordes. Then the Lorraine Crosby Junior High School in Hitchcock was looking for a librarian, and she went to work there because she knew the Dewey Decimal System. She moved up from there to the Hitchcock High School library where she retired after nineteen years.

We eventually had a boy we called Joey, which gave us five children altogether; Teresa, the oldest, Betty and Lisa, the twins, Cathy, and Joey.

Building a Racetrack

Mr. Mecom came to the ranch three or four weeks later and said, "We need to build a race track."

And I said, "Okay, I know where I can get the plans for it."

He said, "Where is that?"

I said, "Tommy Oliphant's got one. It's a five-eighths-of-a-mile track, seventy feet wide, with a three hundred and sixty yard straight-away."

He said, "Oh, that'll be ideal. Can you get those plans for me?"

I said, "Sure can!"

So, he flew me down to Tommy Oliphant's. Everywhere I went with Mr. Mecom we flew. He treated me like royalty. I never met a nicer man in all my life. He had the money, but he treated people with respect all the time.

We got the race track sorted out, and then we decided that we needed a barn. We only had three race horses at the time, and they were in the cow barn with the show cattle, so we had a twenty-four stall barn built, and as the welder, Mr. Howard, was building it, he asked me how high I wanted the shed row. I was on a horse at the time, and I put my hand about a foot or so above my head. "Soupy," I said, "That's how I want it, about that high." And that's how that shed row was built. It's still standing, and in good shape today.

My Television Debut

In 1963 I had a phone call from Arthur Tiner back in Fort Worth. He said they were making a film that Sunday to be shown on Monday at the start of the *Today Show*. He wanted me to ride in a three-hundred-and-fifty-yard match race for the show. It was filmed on the grounds where the TV show *Dallas* was later filmed. So, that Monday morning, my wife got to watch me ride in a race on TV. Too bad there are no photos of that.

Off to the Races

One day in 1964, Mr. Mecom came to me and asked, "You want to go off to the races to train?"

I said, "Yeah."

He said, "I want to send you to Raton, New Mexico."

"Where's Raton, New Mexico?" I asked.

He said, "You'll know when you get there."

So, I went to Raton, New Mexico, with six horses, and stayed there for the full season, which lasted for four months. I ran in twenty-seven races, had eight wins, fifteen places, and won the 4th of July Futurity Race. I had pictures of me in the winner's circle with the blanket and everything, but I sent them to my father and to Mr. Heath, and now they're gone.

La Mesa Park — Raton, New Mexico

Horse racing in the New Mexico Rockies, "The Land of Enchantment". Cool summer climate. Excellent fishing in Lakes and streams within a 60 mile radius of "La Mesa Park Racetrack". Golf course nearby. Horse racing Saturdays, Sundays & Holidays mid May through September, also Fridays, July & August. Two 5000 foot grass landing strips adjacent to parking lot.

Color photo by: Don Sheehan, Raton, New Mexico
57508-B

This postcard from May 1964 from Ron to Patsy reads: "Dear Sweetheart, Here is the race track where I will be racing horses. It is really nice. I thought I would let you know that you have still got a husband and _____ absence makes the heart grow fonder. Well I am really in love with a woman who is a long ways away. Goodnight, _____ XXXXXXXXXXXX

About this time, my sister got in trouble. She charged up a bunch of money on my Texaco credit card—twenty-three hundred dollars—and I was only making a hundred and twenty-seven dollars every two weeks, so I got in touch with Texaco and told them my situation, and they said, "Well, if you can pay it within nine months, we won't charge you any interest."

I didn't know how I was going to pay that money, so I went to Beaman Lee. He was another trainer up the road in Santa Fe, Texas, just up the road from Hitchcock, and I said, "Look, I'm in trouble. I need to make some extra cash. Can I ride some of your horses?"

He said, "You're real lucky, because my jockey has gone to Ruidosa and I need a jockey right now. I can give you fifty cents a ride to gallop the horses."

On the weekends I would ride in races for two dollars—sometimes five dollars for the big races. I was exercising twelve to fifteen head in the morning for Mecom, and turning around and going to ride another ten at night for Beaman Lee. Then on the weekends, I was riding in races. That's how I met some of the bush track jockeys around Texas—riding those weekend races.

After about three months, I said, "Beaman, I can't go no more. I've had it."

And he said, "I'll tell you what, you've been so good," and he gave me the twenty-three hundred dollars I needed to pay off that debt.

Ron winning aboard a horse named "Drag" at Arcadia Downs in Arcadia, Texas June 2, 1963.

I never forgot that. I met another jockey one time. He was broke and didn't have anything, so I put him up in a little motel called the Bostonian, filled his gas tank, and gave him twenty dollars—actually, he owed me quite a bit of money at the time, and I figured I'd never see the rest of that money.

I think it was eight years later, he came back and said, "Here's a hundred dollars."

I said, "What for?"

And he said, "That's for what you did for me. I'm doing great now, I'm in the big time now on the big track and everything."

You know, you have to have trust in somebody.

Chapter 8—The Circle of Life

While I was in New Mexico, my wife, Patsy, was back in Hitchcock, Texas, expecting a baby. She called me and said it was pretty close to the time, so I came down by train from New Mexico. We had Joey on the 11th of August. I held my baby son in my arms at 6:00 that morning and by 8:00 a.m., I was on the train again heading back to Raton, New Mexico.

I'm very proud of the man my son has grown into. Joey married Penelope, his sweetheart from high school. They were both about 18 years old. They had a daughter called Megan, and she now works for the Katy School District, and she married Daniel Chriss, and they have a son named Reed.

Joey started out working for a building company, and then he went to work for Brown and Root. After that, he got a job at the Department of Corrections in Huntsville where he stayed for 10 years. Then he worked for quite a few years selling cars.

At some point, Daniel Chriss, Joey's son-in-law, went to work for a concrete raising company, and he got Joey a job there too. Joey worked his way up in the company to the position of manager and when the owner retired, Joey and Daniel bought the company. They're doing very well now.

Today, Joey and Penelope have started over, and have three smaller children, Joshua, Aiden, and Grace.

Joshua, Joey, Aiden, Ron, and Penelope Kenney at Ron's 80th birthday party.

I got back to Raton, and received a telegram at the Park Plaza Hotel where I was staying. It said that my mother had passed away that same day at 3:00

p.m. English time. I decided that I'd go to church, because I knew my mother would love for me to say a prayer for her. She was pretty religious. She'd been a Captain in the Salvation Army and she was very dedicated to that role, so I went into a church and sat down and picked up a Catholic Missal. It wasn't a Bible, it was a Missal. I had not chosen a Catholic church in particular, but that is where I ended up.

I was flipping through the pages looking for something to read when a couple of ladies came and said, "Hello. Can we help you?"

I told them about my mother dying and me looking for a prayer to read for her.

They said, "We're going to say the rosary. Would you like us to dedicate it to your mother?"

I said, "Thank you. I'd appreciate it." I didn't understand one word they were saying when they said the rosary.

Three days later, my wife received a christening gown, blanket and boots that my mother had crocheted. They were blue.

After I got back from New Mexico, I joined the Catholic Church. My wife and all of her kin folks were Catholics and the children were too, but that's not why I joined that church. I did it because Mother would have wanted me to.

Ten years later, I went back to England and told my older sister how Joey's birth and our mother's death on the same day at nearly the same hour had led me back to religion.

She said, "Well, God moves in mysterious ways, because your mother was born a Catholic, and at seventeen she was baptized as a Catholic, but when she married our dad, she gave up the Catholic religion."

Megan, her husband Daniel Chriss and Ron at his 80th birthday party. Reed Chriss, Aiden, Joshua, and Gracie Kenney.

Chapter 9—The Life of a Jockey

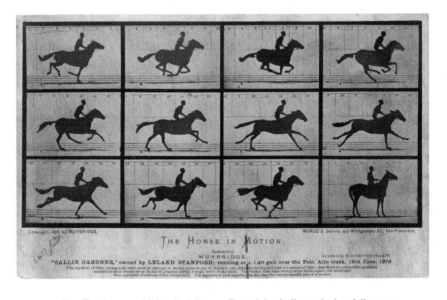

By Eadweard Muybridge—Provided directly by Library of Congress Prints and Photographs Division, Public Domain,
https://commons.wikimedia.org/w/index.php?curid=57260211

When I was getting ready for a race and I needed to drop some weight, I would live on dry toast and tea. No sugar in the tea, just a little cream. And

I do that now, I still drink my tea that way, and I'd just eat dry toast. And that was it. The weight would just melt off. I took my raincoat with me, and I'd run maybe two or three miles. And I'd sweat just like a horse after you've run him. When I came to this country, I weighed a hundred pounds. I would be a hundred, a hundred-and-two in the morning when I'd weigh myself, and by the time I was done I was down to ninety-four pounds from running in my raincoat and eating nothing but dry toast and tea.

Racing is different in England and America. In England, you can't ride in a race unless you belong to the Jockey Club, and as an apprentice comes up through the ranks of apprenticeship, he'll work his way up by riding in apprenticeship races. I beat Lester Piggott in one of those races one day.[15] This horse, Freevale, had never run in a flat race so it was an apprentice race with horses that had never won a race, and he was a five-year-old. I never thought we'd win it, but we won the race. It was the only flat race he had ever run. (A flat race doesn't have any jumps.)

America has mostly all flat racing, but there are still some steeplechases in Kentucky and Maryland. They go fox hunting around there too, but with a

15 Lestor Piggott is a retired English jockey widely regarded as one of the greatest flat racing jockeys of all time with 4,493 career wins.
    Wright, Howard (1986). The Encyclopedia of Flat Racing. Robert Hale. pp. 221–222. ISBN 0-7090-2639-0.

false fox. They place the scent on a piece of cloth, and someone goes out in the morning to trail that scent along the ground. The hounds have to run, so they go down and start at a certain place. Then, of course, the horses follow.

What is a Handicap?

The thing is that the horse's handicap was set at five stone two—a stone is fourteen pounds—so that makes 72 pounds. Well, me, I was so light as an apprentice that they'd have to put three pounds of lead in the saddle to make up that weight. The way they determine how much weight a horse should carry depends on how well the horse has done. Say this horse has won two races, at a certain class; he would have to carry more weight than a horse that hadn't won any races. According to the handicap, the horses should finish all in a straight line. But, of course, it never works that way.

In Steeplechasing, it's different. the lowest weight is 130 pounds for the Steeplechase. When I rode in those races, I rode on the biggest saddle which weighed eight or nine pounds, but someone could still ride the little pound-and-a-half saddle if he was overweight. It's normally a two-mile long race, but for the big races like the Grand National, it might be as long as four miles.

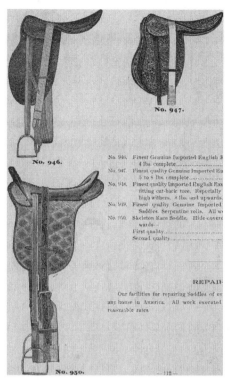

No. 946. Finest Genuine Imported English R
4 lbs. complete................................

No. 947. Finest quality Genuine Imported En
5 to 8 lbs. complete..............................

No. 948. Finest quality Imported English Exc
fitting cut-back tree. Especially
high withers, 8 lbs. and upwards.

No. 949. Finest quality Genuine Imported
Saddles. Serpentine rolls. All wo

No. 950. Skeleton Race Saddle. Hide-covere
wards—
First quality..
Second quality....................................

REPAIR

Our facilities for repairing Saddles of ev
any house in America. All work executed
reasonable rates.

Because of Ron's light weight, he rode the heaviest saddle. Photo originally from the 1892 G.S.Ellis & Son Catalog.

A hurdle race is different altogether. The jumps are sheep panels with birch laced through them to cover them up. They're six-foot-two inches tall, and they lean, and the horse goes over that. It's faster than the Steeplechase. They only have eight jumps in a two mile hurdle race. Whereas a Steeplechase has thirteen jumps with one water jump and one ditch. It covers from two to four-and-a-half miles. Compare that with something like the Kentucky Derby, which is a mile and three eighths, I think. The English ones, they're 1000 guineas (2000 guineas is a mile). The English

Derby is a mile and a half and St. Leger Stakes is a mile, six furlongs, and one hundred and fifteen yards. The horses in the U.S. don't run that far.

And racing Quarter Horses is a different sort of racing entirely. Quarter Horses break out of the gate very fast but they can't run the distance a Thoroughbred can run. The Quarter Horse will run faster than anything for 440 yards—below 24 seconds. I think they're going around 22.2 seconds now, as a matter of fact. Thoroughbreds are even doing that now at the first quarter. How they do that, I don't know. But see, the difference is that the Quarter Horse fades at the finish. He puts everything he has in upfront, and he's got nothing left at the end of a longer race. That's why you see some of these horses that are back runners. A back runner can really come forward at the finish, because they've got the speed to come in at the finish.

So, it is up to the trainer to work out what each horse is good at. Then, you see, this trainer wants to take that back runner and bring him down to make him a Steeplechaser or a hurdler. You don't want him bursting out of the gate, so you start off by doing road work on him, you take him on the road and you don't even show him the gallops. He calms down and he's more relaxed, and then you put him on the gallops and you train him to go two miles. That's very different from the Quarter Horses that are so high-strung when they're young and first broke, you can just barely get hold of them.

The Quarter Horse trainers have taken these young horses and breezed them. This is basically letting the horse run as fast as it wants to go. Let's say the horse is going to run this Sunday. They'll gallop him a little bit Monday. On Tuesday they trot him up, around 200 yards or more. Then they turn him around and walk him on the walking machine for the next two days, so by Friday, they might take him around and gallop and breeze again, so he's all worked up, he doesn't know what to do. So, that's how you do it. But you know, I had one Quarter Horse that was left for me when I was in Raton, New Mexico, and I won with him, and I took him out that same morning and I breezed him three hundred yards. Because over there, you'd sweat like mad. They said, "You're crazy." I ran him in the afternoon in a four-hundred yard race, and he won because he'd settled down.

A four-horse, mechanical horse walker.
photo licensed under the Creative Commons Attribution-
Share Alike 4.0 International license.

Chapter 10—The Horses

Huskey

Huskey was a four-year-old when he came to Mr. Heath's stables. He had won some races on the flats and took to jumping easily and won five races in a row. In his last race he carried a hundred and sixty pounds. Then the next three races nothing—not even a place. So, Mr. Heath got the vet take a look at him. He could not find a thing wrong with the horse except that he was losing a little weight, even though he was still eating good. Then the Blacksmith came to shoe him and found the horse would not let him do anything with his front feet, so Mr. Heath got the vet back with an x-ray, which was not a small machine in those days. He found that Huskey had a small bone, the navicular bone, decayed in each front foot. Although he could walk and even trot on it, that was the end of his racing career. He spent the rest of his life as a pleasure horse for the family.

Malcolm Smith holds a horse named Majestic King in the top photo. In the bottom photo, Ron is looking over the left stall door beside Corny Barry with Tim Farnsworth.

Bonny Silver

Bonny Silver came to us as a four-year-old that had never raced. He belonged to a young girl who used to sing. She was fox hunting with him as well. He was like a spoiled baby; I think he had a brain better than a person, and he won his first two hurdle races just by going out in front and staying there, but that was it. We found out if you whipped him, he stopped. And I mean *stopped*. But he was a big baby. I would try to clean his stall and he kept getting in the way, so I would open his stable door and tell him to get out in the stable yard and wander around until I had finished his stall. Then when I was done, I would say, "alright you can come in now," and in he would come. We knew that he had a lot of speed, because he beat the other horses on the gallops, so Mr. Heath entered him in a novice flat race (that is a race for horses that have never won a flat race) and it was in Edinburgh, three hundred miles away, so it meant an overnight stay. There were six runners, and I rode Bonny Silver. I was told not to use the whip. We were in second place until about two hundred yards from the finish, so I said, "Okay, Bonny lets go," and I talked to him all the way to the finish won by four lengths. But that was the last race for him. After that, he went back to the fox hunting.

Freevale

Freevale was another horse that did not race until he was four years old. He was the most honest horse I think we ever had, though he was not a big stakes winner. He still won twenty-seven Steeplechase races and one flat race. They put him in an apprentice race so I could get a ride. That was when I rode against Lester Piggott. It was a mile and a half, and we won it. That was on Monday, and in Birmingham on Saturday, he ran at Sandown Park in a two-and-a-half-mile Streeplechase and won that too. I could not ride him at home as he was too much horse for me.

The horse in this photo is Teetotal, but that is not Ron on his neck.

Teetotal

A selling placer run in a two-mile Steeplechase race, he was seven years old when we got him in a claiming race. He was not the best looking horse, but he won twelve races in any case. He even won his last race at sixteen years old. He lived to be twenty-seven years old, and he loved people. His owner, Mr. Scarlett, had a stall and five acres of land just for him and a man to look after him until he died.

Fala Tabue

Fala Tabue was the first Quarter Horse that I broke in America at Tommy Oliphant's place at Sabinal. He was easy to break. You could loose-rein him or neck-rein him. When he kicked in, he just left them. The first time I broke out of the gates on him, I think I wound up sitting on his tail. He won the Kansas Futurity, and he won all his trials for the All-American Futurity,[16] but he was poisoned three days before the race. A reward of ten thousand dollars was offered for information, and that was a lot of money in 1960, but they never found out who did it.

---

16 The All American Futurity is run each year at Labor Day at Ruidosa Downs in New Mexico. It is the richest race in America for Quarter Horses and currently boasts greater than $2 million in prize money. The first running of the All American Futurity for two year olds was in 1960. The race covers 440 yards of flat dirt track. It is particularly challenging for young horses due to the altitude. http://www.raceruidoso.com/all-american-futurity2

Two Steeplechasers in the pasture at Mr. Heath's.

Chapter 11—All Good Things Come to an End

In October of 1966, following Joey's birth, I had returned to Texas following the racing season in New Mexico. I studied up and got my U.S. citizenship. This one day, I was trying to break a four-year-old horse. It was being used as a stud by Mr. Mecom down at Laredo. To cut the long story short, I decided this day was not a good day to put an English saddle on this horse, so I put a western saddle on him to try and break him.

Luck was with me, I guess. I took him to the round pen and Jesse Davis gave me a leg up onto the horse. Then the horse stood there, and stood there. I kicked him, and tried to get him to move forward, but instead of going forward, he reared straight up and fell over backwards pinning me underneath the fence.

I can't remember anything more of that day, to tell you the truth. I was knocked out for three solid days. They say that Jesse Davis actually picked the horse up off of me and got me to the shed row and called the ambulance for me.

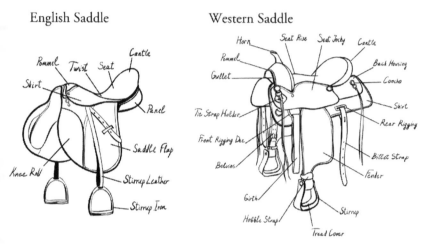

English Saddle   Western Saddle

The larger pommel on the western saddle probably saved Ron's life.

My thigh was broken, and my stomach was ripped open, but the western saddle with its big pommel saved me. If it had been an English saddle there would have been more serious damage. They said I came to three or four times during the days I was unconscious, but I don't remember. I've still got a pin and two metal plates in my leg. The repairs were done remarkably well.

I was out of work until after Christmas. Mr. Cook, the ranch foreman, tried to bring little jobs over to me like saddles and bridles and stuff for me to clean, so I'd be doing something rather than just sitting. I couldn't do the work I was meant to be doing because I was on crutches, and that made me feel worse. Still, I didn't sit and do nothing, I studied to get my United States Citizenship, and I passed that test and became an American citizen.

The week before Christmas, we didn't get a check from Mr. Mecom, and I called Mr. Cook. He said, "Oh no, you've got to go on compensation and you will be getting a check in the New Year."

I said, "Whoa! I can't do that." I thought, *What are we going to live on?* My wife couldn't believe it. *What were we going to do for Christmas?* I called Lannie Mecom,[17] Mr. Mecom's daughter. I had her personal phone number; not many people did.

She said, "Come up to the office in Houston on Monday and we'll talk about it."

When my wife and I got there, Mr. Mecom was there and he asked what the problem was. I told him, and he called Mr. Cook in afterwards.

He told Mr. Cook—straight in front of me— "Give this man his check every month plus give the money he is going to get for compensation, because if you don't, he could sue me, and I could lose quite a lot of money."

I couldn't drive for a while. Altogether I was off for about six months. When I went back, I got

17 The Institute of Texas Cultures recorded an interview with Lannie Mecom Moses for their "Los Tejanos" exhibition in 2015. The video gives a good perspective of this no-nonsense woman who talks about ranching and raising horses and cattle on her ranch, Las Corralitos in Laredo, Texas. https://vimeo.com/129977437

on a horse, and I was very, very nervous. I managed one time around the race track, and I said, "I won't break any more horses," but I would still ride a little bit. Mr. Cook hired another man named Johnny Longdon.

Mr. Mecom kept hiring people. I was still the trainer and still tried to do the work. But this man came in and tried to take over. He and I didn't get along, and one Monday morning he said to me, "You better gallop them horses!"

I said, "Yeah, I'll gallop 'em when I'm ready to gallop 'em!"

And he said, "No, you're going to gallop 'em now."

I told him, "I am still the trainer until I'm told differently by Mr. Mecom, not Mr. Cook or Mr. Longdon." I thought about it a little bit, then I said, "I'll tell you what, you can have this job. I quit!" And that was around about 9:00 in the morning.

Chapter 12—Pat (Parish) Cole Again

Pat Parish in about 1965.

My wife, Patsy, said to me, "What on earth are we going to do now?" Her salary alone wasn't enough with five kids. The only thing I could think to do was to call Pat Parish.

She said, "I'm working at the Lakeside Country Club, come on. There is work here for you too."

I went up there. That phone call took place at 10:00 a.m., so I was never really out of work. Good ol' Pat.

Pat (Parish) Cole's Recollections
of Ron Kenney (continued)

Buster and I moved back to Houston and opened Salt Grass Saddlery and Ron moved into the old house up on Brittmoore Road where he continued to look after our horses for a time. Of course, it wasn't his sort of work, and after a while, millionaire John Mecom hired him to train his thoroughbred race horses. After that, I didn't see Ron for quite a while.

During that time, Bo's Hope, was bred to Triple Chic, a well known Quarter Horse stallion. Bo had a fine little black, bald-faced filly. We called her Triple Hope. Imagine our horror when Bo's Hope dropped dead when the filly was just two weeks old. We ended up raising her on oatmeal mush. To say she was spoiled would be an understatement.

Pat holding Bo's Hope with new baby Triple Hope

I was operating Lakeside Country Club Stables, when who should appear but Ron Kenney. He went to work for me there, and moved into the trainer's house out there.

We had some fun there at that country club stables. Pat was kind of down in the dumps since she and Buster were getting a divorce. I'd get a baked potato and we'd split it in half and Pat and I would share that for our lunch. And when it was hot in the middle of the day, we'd sit in the office and play spite and malice with three decks of cards.

Pat had two orphan fillies at the same time out there. One of them, Triple Hope, turned around to become a champion show horse. She was the daughter of Bo's Hope, the mare Pat and Buster first brought to me to break when I was at Tommy Oliphant's. Well, Bo's Hope died when this filly was two weeks old, so they raised her on a bottle. I broke that filly, and I got her to the point where I could just throw the reins down and let her gallop around the ring and I'd be able to move her with my foot one way or the other way.

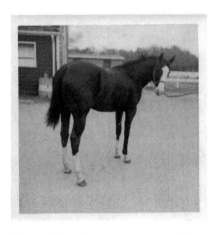

Triple Hope as a two year old.

Triple Hope was really spoiled. She lived in the stall right next to the Coke machine, and she loved strawberry soda. So, the kids that kept their horses there at the country club thought this was the funniest thing, and they'd buy that filly sodas. Pat told everybody not to give her sodas, but they did it anyway. We could always tell because she was black with what they call a bald face—white face and mouth—and that soda dyed her muzzle bright pink. She'd hear the kids put money in the Coke machine and rattle her feed bucket until somebody bought her a drink.

Pat and the people at Lakeside Country Club were very good to me, but most of the horses there were riding horses and show horses for children. It wasn't really my thing. I worked for them for a while until I went on a Catholic retreat.

By this time, I had joined the men's club at the Catholic Church, then I joined the choir, then I joined the Knights of Columbus. I became the Grand Master twice, then I became a fourth degree Knight. The Knights of Columbus help by raising money for the church and for the community, and they also raise money for different causes. For example, when the other beneficial organizations may need help meeting a goal, the Knights of Columbus will donate to them. The fourth degree Knights have more ceremonial duties and stand guard at the caskets at funerals and parades as representatives.

Ron wearing the ceremonial uniform of a fourth degree
Knight of Columbus.

You know, it's funny how people keep popping up in your life. The next time we met, Pat Parish had divorced her husband and moved away. For about seven or eight years I never heard anything about where she was or what she was doing. Then one day in the early eighties, I had a phone call.

She said, "I'm in Madisonville now and I'm married to a man named Jack Cole. We live on a ranch up here and I'd like you to come up and see us sometime."

I said, "Okay," and I went up there and found out that they were operating a business called Metal Concepts, and they were doing well. I tell you what, she married a really wonderful person. Jack was a really, really, nice man. He and I got along really well. For several years after that, I'd keep going up to see them every so often. And then, all of a sudden, I heard Jack had passed away.

Pat and Jack Cole, 1986

Pat asked me to come and sing an Irish song at his funeral, "Danny Boy," which he loved. I was pleased to do it, but it was a very sad occasion.

Then, all of a sudden, Pat was gone again. I didn't know where she'd gone, but out of the blue, she called and said, "I've got a yacht. I'll come to Galveston to pick you and Patsy up if you want me to." And that was as much as we said.

I never got there, but New Year's Eve, 2007, Kim invited me to a New Year's Eve party, and there was Pat again, just the same as always. It was like we had never missed all those years. And that is when we began to discuss putting together a book about my life.

Pat, her daughter Kim, and Ron on New Years Eve, 2007.

Chapter 13—New Directions, Tin Smelting

While I was working with Pat at Lakeside Country Club, I went on a Catholic retreat, and I met a man there called Tom Mackey. He said, "Why don't you give up these horses and come work at the plant?"

I said, "Well, who are you?"

He says, "I'm Tom Mackey. I'm President of the Wah Chang plant, (the tin smelter), in Texas City."

I said, "Okay." I worked for them for nine years and eight months. I was a foreman for seven years until 1976 when the plant was just about closed down. They had reduced each shift from fifteen men down to five men, which meant that they did not need a foreman to manage only five men. The day supervisor could run them. They gave me three months' notice to find another job. They were not going to pay me what I had put into the retirement fund, because they said I had not made it to ten years on the job.

The Wah Chang Tin Smelter

Texas City, Texas

In 1948, the Longhorn Tin Smelter in Texas City was the only tin smelter in the United States. In 1957, the Wah Chang Smelting and Refining Corporation bought the plant from the US government. In the 1940s the plant had over 800 employees and produced 43,500 long tons of tin per year, or 45 percent of world production. By the end of Ron's time there in 1976, the plant had changed hands several times, and production was dramatically reduced.

"Texas State Historical Association (TSHA)." The Handbook of Texas Online| Texas State Historical Association (TSHA). Accessed May 12, 2018. http://www.tshaonline.org/handbook/online/articles/TT/dkt1.html.

I looked all over for another job. I had permission to leave at any time to look for work, but while I was there, I had a close call with death in the form of chlorine gas. A tank car was leaking gas, and some men were working downstream of the tank car. I tried on three different gas masks and all the cylinders were empty, so I put a handkerchief over my mouth and went in and closed off the valve. Well, I still got gassed and landed in the hospital for four days, and I was off work for about two weeks. They had to pump some sort of liquid down into my lungs to spare them from gas burns.

In the end, though, a lawyer named Mr. Birvallhamer got in touch with the head office in Chicago and they finally sent me what I had paid into the retirement fund, so when I went to work at Amoco, I had paid off my house and car, and I was debt free.

Tin Smelting Plant, Texas City, Texas

I should mention that during these years I did other things besides just working. I started coaching children's soccer teams in Hitchcock, Santa Fe, and LaMarque, Texas. Mr. Armanderas and I introduced soccer in that area. We joined the Bay Area Soccer Association. At the time the Bay Area Soccer Association had about seven hundred teams. Now they have over four thousand. Still today, children I coached come up to me, with their children and ask if I remember them.

Also during this time, I got my GED, at Tom Mackey's suggestion. I even went on and got twenty-one college credit hours at Texas A&M. With Tom Mackey's help, that is how I made foreman at the tin smelter.

Chapter 14—Starting Again at Amoco

Since 1964, I'd been bowling on a team captained by Dominique Tebaldo, owner of the feed store where I bought all of the horse feed for Mr. Mecom. When I was in town, I bowled with them. There was a time when I didn't have the money to bowl, so Dominique paid for me and always gave me eighty cents to get in the pot games too. When I got laid off at the tin smelter, I was talking to the others we bowled with about how I may have to go back to working with horses again because I was getting laid off. I told the team that I wasn't sure I would be able to keep bowling with them the next season.

I was 46 years old at the time, and I said, "Whoa! You know, this is starting over fresh!"

A man called Don Hanson said to me, "I'll tell you what, on Sunday night at 8:00, go to the Amoco plant and talk to the guard. He will give you a form to fill out." We were bowling together on Wednesday.

I said, "Okay," and I went over there on the Sunday, filled the form out and handed it back to the guard. Monday morning at 9:00 a.m. I got a call to come for an interview.

You know how fate always happens to some people? It turned out that three of my interviewers were people I was bowled with. I got the job at Amoco.

I had to go to classes for six weeks, and I was having a hard time in the class. Halfway through the training, I went to see the man, I don't know his full name, but we nicknamed him Fuzzy because he was always scratching his face like he had fuzz on it even though he was clean shaven.

I said, "Fuzzy, it doesn't look like I'm gonna be able to manage this. This schooling is just getting me down."

He said, "Don't worry about it. When you get on the unit, they'll teach you everything you need to know." And they did. I was the oldest one in the class so they sent me to Powerhouse. It was nicknamed the "old folks home." In 1984, Amoco went on strike. The union and the company could not get together on a settlement for four months. While we were out of work, I took small jobs, some for a day, some for two or three days. Like Constable Joe Scrofne once got me a job delivering flowers. The hardest temporary job I had was going out in the boat early in the morning and picking up oysters and bringing them home and shucking them for $20 per gallon. It was very hard work, but we made it. We paid our bills, and after the strike, we still had money in our checking account. Some jobs I took were $1.80 per hour, but like they say, it put bread on the table.

Ron had no trouble with the job once he got on the unit. He worked with "Powerhouse," nicknamed "the old folks home." They are pictured here at the bottom left.

I worked for 14 years and 8 months with Amoco and they treated me very well.

During his time at Amoco, Ron was
honored with several awards.

I retired from Amoco in 1992, at the age of 62,
and I loved working there. My wife Patsy gave me a
retirement party at the Knights of Columbus Hall on
Delany Road. Three or four hundred people came.

Society Spotlights

Ron Kenney was honored with a
retirement party on Sunday, Oct. 4 at
the Knights of Columbus Hall on
Delany Road in La Marque. He retired
after 13 years with Amoco Oil.

The party was given in his honor
by his wife, Patsy, and children, Teresa, Betty, Lisa, Cathy and Joey.
Approximately 125 relatives and
friends attended the event.

After a three-week vacation to
England, his home, he will be enjoying his main hobbies, fishing, bowling
and gardening.

Ron and Patsy at Ron's Retirement Party

Ron when he retired in 1992 at the age of 62.

Chapter 15—Hayes Funeral Home, My Lifeline

In April 1993, I was helping Father John Defork with some funerals in role of an Argonot, when Mrs. Lynn Hayes asked me if I would like to work for them. At first, I didn't think I wanted to work for a funeral home. But I thought more about it and decided to give it a try. I think I would have gone crazy if it had not been for Allen and Barbara Hayes. They treat me like family, and all the people that work for them. There is so much Allen and Barbara have done for me. It would fill a lot more pages.

My step-daughter Cathy passed away December 2, 2003, of cancer and that was when Patsy's health really started going down. She died March 31, 2006 and left a big hole in my life. We'd been married for forty-three years, and I didn't know if I was coming or going. If it hadn't been for the Hayes family and dear Betty Armstrong I don't know what I would have done. Betty was a devoted friend who was always calling and coming by to make sure that I was okay. Then on July 22, 2007, Betty died and left me as well.

I didn't know what to do. I was, and still am, on a fixed income, and I tried to stay on in my house, but it was too big for me, and it held too many memories. I moved into the Lakeview Apartments in Texas City. I still had my part-time job at Hayes Funeral Home. Thank goodness! Once I left my house, I had no yard work, nothing to fix, no neighbors, and not even my little dog to talk to. The rent went up and Hurricane Ike came through, which messed up my apartment, so I had to move. The Hayes had a small rental property that came available, and that meant I could move back to my home town of Hitchcock, Texas. My friends came to help me move, and by this time I was seeing my son Joey and his family a lot more, but I felt lonely.

I have made some great friends in Texas, and they have helped me to hold my life together, because I really did not want to live anymore. My friends the Hayes even took me with them on a cruise, where I had fun in spite of myself. I went to church, sang in the choir, bowled, joined the Lions Club and went to game rooms to play and talk. I continued to watch sports and work puzzles, but I was far from feeling satisfied.

Barbara and Allen Hayes on a trip to England with Ron in 2006.

I joined the Sante Fe Lions Club after I was asked to give a talk about my life in England. A man named Cotton Miller invited me. I was happy to join when I learned what the Lions do, like helping low income people to get glasses, training seeing-eye dogs, running a free camp in Kerrville, Texas, for disabled children, and doing many other things for their local communities as the need arises.

Ron Kenney is a man short in stature but tall in tales. His small size as a child dictated what he was "chosen" to do in England, but his dreams were far bigger. He brought those big dreams to the United States of America where his small size allowed him to stand tall. Ron soared to new heights as a young man competing as a horse jockey. He went on from there to marry and raise a family and live a successful life full of wonderful stories and lessons learned.

I personally have come to know Ron in the later chapters of his life since he came to work for my husband, Allen, at our family owned funeral home. He is a ball of energy and enthusiasm—always up to any challenge. We quickly became fishing buddies and the fish tales grow bigger every time we tell them. Ron makes me laugh and appreciate life at any age.

I believe that people of all ages will enjoy reading Ron's life story of struggles and triumphs. He is a perfect example of an American success story— someone who has risen above it all to stand tall and proud. His heart of gold and never-failing determination have molded his life and made him a giant in my books!

Dr. Barbara Hayes
DNP, FNP-C

I met Mr. Ron Kenney when I began working at Hayes Funeral Home in 2011. He has always been a kind and giving man to me and my two children. He has attended my daughter's dance recitals. He told her how good she did, made sure my son could play soccer and asked on a weekly basis how he was doing. He brought them fishing poles so they could fish. He pretty much just stepped in as a surrogate grandfather, which means a lot since their grandparents are deceased. Ron brings us "girls" candy at work and makes sure we have lunch. He always has a smile on his face and a song on his lips. He has blessed mine and my children's lives and I am so glad that the Lord saw fit to bring him into our lives.

Sharon Lofgren
Hayes Funeral Home
Hitchcock, Texas

Chapter 16—Dancing Back to Life

In 2010, I was talked into going to the Galveston County Fair and Rodeo Senior Day with a group through the Catholic church called "Friends." It was made up of women and men over the age of 62. Senior day had free barbecue sandwiches, bingo, prizes, music, and even a dance contest. A friend named Sadie and her husband knew a lady who had come with a different group that day, The Galveston Grandmother's Club #277. This lady asked Sadie if there might be a man at our table who would like to dance, and Sadie said she thought there just might be, so she walked back to the table and asked. Apparently, so they tell me, I jumped up and ran over there and asked this mystery woman her name.

"Alice Keel," she said.

I told her, "My name is Ron, but I can't stay and dance because I have to leave to go to work." It turned out that Alice had been a widow since 1997.

She was content with her life, unlike me. I was not settled enough to even know what I wanted, but I stood there and asked her if she would like to go to dinner sometime.

To my shock, she said, "yes."

I told her, "I'll call you someday," and I started walking off.

She called me back and said, "You would need my telephone number to call me." At this point, she was not sure about me, she asked for *my* telephone number and said, "I will call you."

A few days went by. No call. I searched the telephone books for her name but could not find it.

Later, she told me she was not sure about calling, but something inside her told her to make the call. I will never forget, I was in choir practice, and everyone kidded me about a lady calling me. She told me she would call me back after choir practice—I did not want to hang up!

A long two hours later Alice called again and asked if I still wanted go out to eat. I said, "Yes! Where do you live?"

We talked a while and she suggested we go back to the Fair and Rodeo and eat, then watch the Rodeo. I agreed, and she asked where I lived. She said she'd pick me up and that we would be meeting her brother Albert and his girlfriend out there. I wanted to pick her up, but she told me no, because she did not know me well enough. I think that is why we joined her brother. We had a good time and we talked about dancing. I told her I could not dance then corrected myself to say—I had not danced in a lot of years, since my wife and I had not danced well together.

Alice asked me if I would like to go to a dance and try. You see, her other brother, Henry, and his wife hosted a Young Adults Handi Cap dance. Alice said that way if we didn't dance well or looked stupid, no one would know the difference. We wouldn't be embarrassed, plus, her brother would be there too. I guess she still didn't quite trust me. Things went well, and we enjoyed learning to dance with each other. I did really well and tried anything they played.

I enjoyed Alice's company, and I liked her two brothers, too. I wanted to see her some more. Well, she must have felt the same way, because she finally told me where she lived but told me to call first. "Don't just show up!" And she gave me her telephone number.

Alice began to tell me about herself, like how she worked at American National Insurance Company, and had done so for over 35 years. She also had a part-time job at Highlands Baptist Church in La Marque, Texas, where she taught and watched the young children and babies. She told me about her family, two grown daughters, two sons-in-law, a grandson in Texas and three grown step-grandchildren living in Florida with six step-great-grandchildren. She had a daughter who was terminally ill with Lupus. Her name was Brenda, the youngest. The oldest daughter has arthritis in her back, and her name is Candye. Alice told me she was very busy with the grown girls, work, and going places when she could. She also had a big family and they were close. She told me she was not sure she had time for a full-time man in her life.

Brian and Brenda Martin and Candye and Eric Brandon, Alice's two daughters and their husbands.

I didn't want to agree with her, but I didn't think it sounded like she had time for me either. I could remember taking care of my wife Patsy, and when you love someone and want to do a good job of looking after them, it takes a lot of time. I also found out that I was much older than Alice. She let me know that she just wanted to go out occasionally and have fun. In other words, I would not be the center of her attention.

Eventually, I guess it worked itself out, because we did start seeing each other, and we did a lot of fun things together—high school football games, plays at the college, shows, musicals, day trips with a group she belonged to. Everything we did, we had fun. Alice had even planned a trip to go to Colorado, and, of course, I got on that trip too, and we had fun the whole time. I started enjoying having fun again.

Alice and Ron in Colorado Springs in 2010.

When we got back from Colorado, I visited her nondenominational church. I had been going through a change of churches myself, from the Catholic church to a Lutheran church. And Alice visited the Santa Fe Lions Club meeting with me. Then she went with me to a church where we had a sing-along of Christian songs. She cooked a big pot of food for the covered dish buffet afterwards.

My family had birthday parties for my grand-children and great-grandchild. I saw my son seemed to like Alice. You could say "they hit it off." Plus, we took her grandson, Nicholas, a few places and I was honored to be invited to his birthday party, where I had a great time, as did the younger boys. In their goodie bags each received a kite, but they really didn't know what to do with them. So, I got to show off and help eight or nine little boys fly kites in the street for the first time. We all had fun. The best thing was that Alice's daughters seemed to like me and I enjoyed their company too. I felt like I fit in, and I felt love between all of us. And you should have seen and heard those boys running down the street, trying to keep the kites up and flying. It was magic.

Ron and Nicholas showing their manlihood by knocking a tree stump down.

Dating Adventures

ALICE: A funny thing happened on the way to look at the Christmas lights in Bryan one day. We stopped at this big dance hall looking place with a restaurant inside it. The owner had hung up lots of pictures of different Western things. Our group went and sat down, and this crippled guy came walking in to the table and he was talking to us while we waited for the waitress to get there, and somebody asked him what had happened to him. He said, all matter-of-fact, "I got injured riding in the rodeo." Well, Ron and I hadn't been together long, and I got up and went to the restroom. The man was saying, "Yeah, I have race horses. In fact, I got a race horse on my wall and there's a jockey that was riding it, but I don't know who the jockey was." About this time, I came out of the restroom and found everybody all crowded together on one side of the room and I thought, *Oh, my! I hope he hasn't started something.* Then I heard Ron say, "Oh! That's me on that horse!"

RON: You could see me as plain as day up on that horse. The man said, "I've been looking a long time for the person who rode that horse." I picked up the race and he didn't have a jockey there and, he came and asked me, and I said, "Yeah, I'll ride him." It was a 350-yard race, and I won that race.

Chapter 17—Life Begins Again at 80

My 80th birthday was coming up and the Hayes were planning a birthday party for me. That was when Alice and I would have to face the age difference between us. I was not sure how Alice would feel about that, but it did not seem to matter. The party brought family and friends together and everybody had a good time. Alice took pictures of me with lots of different people, and that is when I really realized I loved her and she loved me, I hoped, but most of all she cared for me. She gave me a birthday card I will keep with me forever—because there was so much love in it.

The birthday card that Alice gave to Ron when he turned 80.

So, we realized that we wanted to share the rest of our lives together, and before we knew it, we were planning a wedding. We needed a date, it was August, so Alice picked the second of January, her grandmother's birthday. It was going to be a small wedding—a Sunday afternoon get-together. The year was 2011.

Wedding Invitation
A moment to cherish

Ms. Alice Keel
&
Mr. Ronald Kenney

3:00 P.M. ~ Sunday
January 2, 2011
St. John's Lutheran Church
13136 Highway 6
Santa Fe, Texas 77510

Come, Come, Casual Dress

No Gifts, Please!!!
Reception to follow wedding ceremony at the church hall   Love,

As we got to know each other and traveled together, I learned quickly about Alice's life. Her youngest daughter became very ill at one point, and we almost lost her. She was sick off and on for several months as I watched Alice go out daily at all hours to care for Brenda. The rest of Alice's immediate family, daughter Candye, grandson Nicholas, both sons-in-laws Brian and Eric, did whatever was needed to help. It was strange to me to see how well Brenda's dad and Alice got along as they took care of whatever needed to be done. That often involved spending time together in the hospital. It worried me a little, because I felt like he had feelings for her still and might like to have his family back, but Brenda's health had improved, and she made plans to move back home to San Antonio. Following those rough times, I got to meet Alice's other brother, Louis, and his wife. They treated us to a nice meal out, and things went well. He seemed to like me.

The wedding planning picked up again, and Brenda came down for New Year's, so the wedding was still happening January 2, 2011. Since the both of us were so patriotic, we decorated with red, white, and blue for a real patriotic wedding and reception. I wore a white tail coat with red and blue cords on the shoulders and a blue shirt. Alice wore a red dress with her mother's white shawl trimmed with red and blue. Two couples stood up with us: the ladies wore light blue with crocheted white shawls, and the men wore dark blue. My two young grandsons, Joey's boys, were ring bearers. They wore red-and-blue striped shirts with blue pants, and Alice's grandson wore dark blue pants and a white shirt.

Jan 2nd 2011

We used the Lutheran church because it was close to where we lived, and it had a gazebo for the service. The part-time pastor, Rosy, was great. As it was January, it could have been cold or raining, and the minister tried to talk Alice into a back-up plan to have the ceremony inside the church, but she would not hear of it. All Sundays were cold with rain that year except the one we got married on.

Alice arrived with her grandson in a limousine provided by Allen and Barbara Hayes. He helped her out and up the stairs where I waited with the minster and the two couples. My two grandsons came up on the stairs right before Alice. I could not believe I was really getting married. The weather was a little chilly, but pretty, and I was getting a new family. I started to feel complete again. It was like life started all over and everyone loved me.

After the service, we headed to the hall, and realized we had invited a lot of guests. Some just showed up when they heard we were getting married.

Inside you could not miss the beautiful cake Betty made. (Betty is Alice's daughters' half sister.) The cake had three big layers on a stand with a water fall all red and blue. It stood taller than us. There were also two groom's cakes—one white and the other chocolate—decorated by Alice. One for my sports and the other a religious one with a cross. On a table was a book with a money tree and a basket for cards. Brenda and Candye, Alice's girls looked after that for us while Betty served her cake. Other friends helped cutting the other cakes and serving the finger foods. We spent a lot of time visiting with everyone and taking pictures. No one was in any hurry to leave, since it was an afternoon wedding that lasted until 8:00 p.m. When it was time for us to leave, my two new sons-in-law saw things got to the house and cleaned everything up.

Alice's brothers at the wedding: Albert Stewart, Alice, Ron, Louis Stewart, and Henry Stewart.

We headed for the big city of Galveston, Texas, to Moody Gardens. Alice had a friend whose daughter worked there, and she got us a good deal on a room with a balcony that had a view of the Christmas light displays over the bay and pools. When we got there, we found a lovely big basket of fruit, wine, and chocolates. We stood on our balcony in the January cold and took in the sights, then we went to the hot tub—yes, it was outside, but the water was hot with steam coming off of it. We laughed and enjoyed the water then ran back inside before we froze to death. The pool inside was supposed to be heated but the heater was broken, so we headed back to our room.

The next day we toured around Moody Gardens and the Kemah Boardwalk. That evening we headed to San Antonio to Alice's daughter's house. The four of us went to a hockey game, and sat right up close to the rink. It was a great time. After a day or two of being gone, we went to Alice's house, now mine too. I had a house paid for again, and work to do to fix it up.

Our next challenge was learning to combine two lives and families into one. We first had to combine two houses worth of stuff, work out what to keep and what to give away and figure out where to put it all.

Our churches have changed, and our faith has grown stronger. We ended up at the College View Church of Texas City. Alice retired from work, but we both have part-time jobs we like. We say that is our fun money. We also do a lot of volunteer work—more since Alice lost her daughter to God. That was a hard battle for us to travel back and forth to San Antonio—also through the hurt of it. After all, I had been through this with Patsy and her daughter. Patsy withdrew from life after her daughter's death and kind of left me out, but thank God Alice had more faith and peace with God taking her Brenda home. It was a difficult time, but together we made it through. I think that is where I learned to hold onto my faith. I learned it from watching Alice.

Combining Families

ALICE: We took my grandson to Disney World and he didn't want to buy any souvenirs. Some candy and ice cream, but he didn't really want any kind of junk, so we went to the airport and I told him to see if he could find anything there that he wanted to take home with him. After a while, he came and said, "I want to get this cup for Ron for his birthday." I looked at it with cartoon characters on it, then I noticed that the handle said "Grandpa" on it. I told my grandson, "You do see that this handle says Grandpa, right?" He said, "Yes." He told me he'd distract Ron while I bought the cup with his money, then he'd give it to him while we waited at the airport.

RON: Nicholas is a great kid.

Don't get me wrong our marriage has had its ups and downs, but I feel and know that Alice loves me for me. My wife seems to fit in with anything I get her into.

Let me tell you about the many things I get Alice into before I close. It is hard at times to know we love each other, because of our differences, but we do love and care about each other. We express it differently because we grew up differently. I did not have the sort of happy childhood Alice had, and she went through a divorce, but I did not. The result was that I sometimes could not understand her feelings about things, but we enjoy our lives together.

We stay busy. We are blessed with good health. We go to church to learn and praise God, which is something new for me. When I used to go to church it was just a service, but now I am learning how to talk to God. We enjoy time with our family and our many friends. We go places to tell my life history in England and to sing. Alice, of course, always cooks a dish or hands out something to everyone.

Ron singing the National Anthem at the Annual Convention of the Grandmother's Club. He's done this for two national conventions, and now holds the office of Secretary for Club #277. He's also sung the National Anthem for a few Lions International Conventions.

We dress and play Mr. & Mrs. Claus, Mr. &
Mrs. Easter Bunny, and two Leprechauns. In those

roles, I often sing, and Alice hands out candy or cookies. There are times we just go to sing patriotic songs and dress up for the event. Alice makes sure we are dressed appropriately.

The Santa Fe Lions Club (where I served as President and Vice President for two years respectively) and the Galveston Grandmothers Club #277 (oldest club in the National Federation of Grandmothers Clubs of America, Inc.) keep us busy doing for the communities. I was proud to be the very first male member of the Grandmothers Club when they decided to allow men to join. Alice has been president of that fine organization four times. They contribute to research relating to children's diseases. Grandmothers Clubs also help out with other causes in the community. Of course they're a nonprofit organization.

Our many voluntary duties in the community might include calling the numbers at bingo, baking, selling raffle tickets, or serving food. We also volunteer at Hitchcock Library and a few churches and other clubs. We have a lot of fun with it. For instance, in Galveston, we volunteer at the Grand 1894 Opera House about 80 hours per year, which means that we get to watch the shows.

We like to return each year to the Fair and Rodeo where we met. We have won in the Dance Contest plus we hand out the first-place belt buckle for the steer contest as representatives of the Lions Club, also we have been in several Hitchcock parades as Mr. and Mrs. Claus. Once, Alice was named

Ron and Alice in their Lions Club Vests.

Miss Golden Girl Queen in The Old Lady Beauty Contest. Bless her heart, my wife keeps up with all this on the calendar so I don't double-book, as I am sure I would! I left a few things out of this list of what we do, but you get the idea. We enjoy having fun helping others.

So, I am really happy with my life, and if God is willing to keep us, we will keep doing it.

Ron and Alice won second place at the dance
competition at the 2017 Galveston County
Fair and Rodeo.

My Husband Acts Like a Horse

ALICE: This is going to sound funny, but when Ron breathes sometimes, he sounds like a horse! I tease him about it, but I really wonder. When he talks about the horses, I see that he's like a race horse. There'll be days when he does a hundred things at 90 miles-a-minute and won't rest then BOOM, the next day he is wiped out.

RON: Well, you see, I got used to getting up in the morning, letting the dogs loose, working the horses, and then in the afternoon, the horses took a break, so I took a break.

ALICE: And he sweats a lot just like a horse after you've run him. He acts a lot like a horse.

A Brief Glossary of Horse Racing Terms

This list is far from exhaustive. I have tried to define the terms that have been used in the text to this point.

Break (A horse)—To accustom a young horse to racing equipment and methods, and to carry a rider.

Breeze—A term generally used to describe a workout in which a horse is easily running under a hold without encouragement from the rider. Also called "working" the horse is when you let the horse run at racing speed.

Bush track—Informal horse races run in rural areas of the United States and southern Canada. Quarter Horses, ridden by amateur jockeys, race on makeshift tracks. Race times are not kept and the track length varies.[18] Some bush tracks are a little more formal, with names and a regular following.

Exercise Riders—work for trainers and ride young horses in training on gallops or training tracks.

Farrier—Blacksmith.

Flat race—Contested on level ground as opposed to hurdle race or steeplechase.

Furlong—One-eighth of a mile; 220 yards; 660 feet.

Gait—The ways in which a horse can move-walk, trot, canter, gallop, run, etc.

Gallop—The gallop is very much like the canter, except it is faster, more ground-covering, and a four-beat gait. It is the

---

18 Drape, Joe. "Love of Racing Grows in the Bushes." The New York Times. March 09, 1997. Accessed May 12, 2018. https://www.ny-times.com/1997/03/09/sports/love-of-racing-grows-in-the-bushes.html.

fastest gait of the horse, averaging about 25 to 30 miles per hour. A gallop may also be a training track.

Gelding—Castrated male horse.

Groom—A person who cares for a horse in a stable.

Handicap—Race for which a handicapper assigns weights to be carried. Also, to handicap a race, to make selections on the basis of the past performances.

Handily—Working or racing with moderate effort, but more effort than breezing.

Hands—The height of a horse is measured in "hands." One hand is about four inches.

Hurdle race—Contested over obstacles. A jumping race over lower fences than those used in the steeplechase races.

Jockey fee—Sum paid to a rider.

Jog—Slow, easy gait.

Jumper—Steeplechase or hurdle horse.

Length—Length of a horse from nose to tail, about 8 feet. Also distance between horses in a race.

Loose Rein—Riding with a loose rein refers to allowing the reins to hang loose. The rider directs the horse using subtle pressure with his legs.

Neck Rein—Riding with a neck rein, the rider turns the horse with the pressure of the rein on his neck rather than direct pressure on a bit.

Quarter Horse—Breed of horse especially fast for a quarter of a mile, from which its name is derived.

Schooling—Accustoming a horse to starting from the gate and to teach him racing practices. In steeplechasing, more particularly to teach a horse to jump.

Shed row—Stable area. A row of barns.

Starting gate—Mechanical device having partitions (stalls) for horses in which they are confined until the starter releases the doors in front to begin the race.

Steeplechase—A jumping race over high obstacles.

Trainers—Appointed by the owners of the horses. A trainer is an individual whose job it is to maximise the potential of each horse in their care. Some trainers train as many as 300 horses at one time.

Training—After breaking-in is completed, horses enter training yards where they prepare for races.

Stable lads or lasses are responsible for the general care and treatment of the horses to ensure that each horse is well looked after. This is referred to as **grooming**.

Training yards—The place where a trainer works with his horses.

Trotting—The second fastest gait of a horse, between a walk and a canter in speed, in which diagonal pairs of legs move forward together.

Work—To exercise a horse. A workout.